CARTESIAN STUDIES

CARTESIAN STUDIES

Edited by

R. J. BUTLER

Professor of Philosophy,
University of Kent at Canterbury

BASIL BLACKWELL
OXFORD
1972

ISBN 0 631 13750 5

Library of Congress Catalog Card Number: 71–149139

PRINTED IN GREAT BRITAIN
BY A. T. BROOME AND SON, 18 ST. CLEMENT'S, OXFORD
AND BOUND BY THE KEMP HALL BINDERY, OXFORD

CONTENTS

PREFACE

This volume has grown out of two Workshops on Descartes held at the University of Waterloo. The first, sponsored by the university, met in April, 1968, and the second, sponsored by the Canada Council, met in October, 1968. The first four papers in this volume and the sixth were given at these Workshops: the remaining three have been contributed subsequently.

The following abbreviations have been used: C. Adam and P. Tannery's *Oeuvres de Descartes* (Paris, 1897–1913) is referred to by 'AT' followed by the volume, and then the page number. C. Adam and G. Milhaud's *Correspondence de Descartes* (Paris, 1926–63) is referred to by 'AM' followed by the volume, and then the page number. *The Philosophical Works of Descartes* translated by E. S. Haldane and G. R. T. Ross (Cambridge, 1911) is indicated by 'HR' followed by the volume and the page number. *Descartes: Philosophical Writings* translated by E. Anscombe and P. T. Geach (London, 1954) is referred to by 'AG' followed by the page number.

I wish to thank the University of Waterloo and the Canada Council for underwriting the Workshops in the first place, and the contributors to this volume for their encouragement and support.

R.J.B.

DESCARTES ON THE WILL

ANTHONY KENNY

The problems I wish to discuss concern two developments which took place, or are alleged to have taken place, in Descartes' teaching concerning the relation of the intellect and the will.

The first is this. In the *Regulae* (AT X, 420) Descartes says that we must distinguish the faculty of the intellect by which it intuits and knows things from the faculty by which it makes affirmative and negative judgements.[1] In the same book he says that belief in revelation, by contrast with science, 'is not an act of the mind but of the will'.[2] On the other hand, in the *Principles of Philosophy* we are told that, while sensation, imagination, and pure intellection are modes of perception, desire and aversion, affirmation, denial and doubt are different modes of willing.[3] This classification of affirmative and negative judgements as an act of will is anticipated in the Fourth Meditation, where he distinguishes the intellect or faculty of knowing (*facultas cognoscendi*) from the will or faculty of choosing (*facultas eligendi*) and says that the intellect merely perceives ideas for judgement[4] and that judgements are acts of the will;[5] the cause of erroneous judgement is the fact that our will extends further than our intellect.[6]

In the same passage of the *Meditations* occurs the sentence which introduces the second of the two contrasts I want to discuss. 'I could not refrain from judging' Descartes says 'that what I so clearly understood was true . . . because from a great light in my intellect there followed an inclination of will.'[7] The assertion that

---

[1] Distinguamus illam facultatem intellectus per quam res intuetur et cognoscit ab ea qua judicat affirmando vel negando.

[2] Non ingenii actio sit sed voluntatis (AT X, 370).

[3] Sentire imaginari et pure intelligere sunt tantum modi percipiendi; ut et cupere aversari, affirmare, negare, dubitare sunt diversi modi volendi (AT VIII, 17).

[4] Per solum intellectum percipio tantum ideas de quibus iudicium ferre possum (AT VII, 50).

[5] Illos actus voluntatis, sive illa iudicia, in quibus fallor (AT VII, 60).

[6] Latius pateat voluntas quam intellectus (AT VII, 50).

[7] Non potui non iudicare illud quod tam clare intelligebam verum esse . . . quia ex magna luce in intellectu magna consequuta est propensio in voluntate AT VII, 59).

the will is determined by the intellect is generalised in the geometrical exposition of the *Meditations* which follows the Second
Objections. 'The will of a thinking substance is impelled—
voluntarily and freely, since that is of the essence of the will, but
none the less infallibly—towards a good clearly known to it.'[8] And
in the reply to the same objections he gives examples of propositions which are so clearly perceived by the intellect that we cannot
think of them without believing them to be true (AT VII, 145).
In a letter perhaps written to Mesland in 1645, on the other hand,
Descartes wrote as follows. 'It is always open to us to hold back
from pursuing a clearly known good, or from admitting a clearly
perceived truth, provided we consider it a good thing to demonstrate the freedom of the will by so doing.'[9]

We have, then, two contrasts. In the *Regulae*, Descartes treats
judgement as an act of the intellect; in later works he treats it as
an act of the will. In the *Meditations* Descartes says that clear
perception determines the will; in the letter to Mesland he says
that clear perception can be rejected by the will. I want to take
each of these contrasts in turn to see how far they represent a real
change of mind in Descartes.

I. *Descartes' Theory of Judgement*

To the modern philosopher, the statement of the *Regulae* that
judgement is an act of the intellect, seems more natural than the
theory of the *Principles* that judgement is an act of the will. A
practical judgement, a decision what to do, may perhaps be
regarded as an act of the will; but a speculative judgement, a
decision that such and such is the case, an assent to a proposition
rather than to a proposal: this seems, if we are to talk of faculties
at all, to belong to a cognitive rather than to an appetitive faculty.
Such too was the opinion of the scholastics of Descartes' time.
To see what he is likely to have been taught by the Thomists of La
Flèche, we may consider the following text of St. Thomas, one of
many quoted in Gilson's *Index Scolastico-Cartesien*. In Ia IIae
17, 6 St. Thomas inquires whether the act of reason can be commanded by the will. He replies as follows. 'Since reason reflects

---

[8] Rei cogitantis voluntas fertur, voluntarie quidem et libere—hoc enim est
de essentia voluntatis—sed nihilominus infallibiliter, in bonum sibi clare
cognitum (AT VII, 166).

[9] Semper enim nobis licet nos revocare a bono clare cognito prosequendo,
vei a perspicua veritate admittenda, modo tantum cogitemus bonum libertatem
arbitrii nostri per hoc testari (AT VI, 197).

on itself, it can order its own acts just as it can order the acts of other faculties; and so its own act can be commanded. But it must be observed that the act of reason can be considered in two ways. First we may consider the exercise of the act: in this sense the act of reason can always be commanded, as when someone is told to pay attention and use his reason. Secondly, we may consider the object of the act; and in this connection there are two different acts of reason to be considered. The first is the apprehension of truth about something, this is not in our power but comes about in virtue of a natural or supernatural light; and so in this respect the act of reason is not in our power and cannot be commanded. But there is another act of reason which consists in assent to what is apprehended. Where what is apprehended is something like the first principles to which the intellect naturally assents, to assent or dissent is not in our power but in the order of nature; and so, strictly speaking, it is at the command of nature. But there are some things apprehended which do not so convince the intellect as to take away its power of assent or dissent; these leave it free at least to suspend its assent or dissent for some cause; and in such cases assent and dissent are in our power and subject to command.'[10]

Any reader of Descartes will notice great similarities between his doctrine and that of St. Thomas. Descartes distinguishes frequently between what we perceive or understand and what we judge: out of many passages, we can quote the letter to Hyper-aspistes; 'I have frequently observed that what men judge to be the case differs from what they really understand to be the case'.[11] Descartes' distinction between perception and judgement corresponds to Aquinas' between apprehension and assent. Like

[10]Respondeo dicendum quod quia ratio supra seipsam reflectitur, sicut ordinat de actibus aliarum potentiarum, ita etiam potest ordinare de suo actu; unde etiam actus ipsius potest esse imperatus. Sed attendendum est quod actus rationis potest considerari dupliciter: uno modo quantum ad exercitium actus, et six actus rationis semper imperari potest, sicut cum indicitur alicui quod attendat, et rationi utatur. Alio modo quantum ad objectum, respectu cujus duo actus rationis attenduntur: primo quidem, ut veritatem circa aliquid apprehendat; et hoc non est in potestate nostra; hoc enim contingit per virtutem alicuius luminis vel naturalis vel supernaturalis. Et ideo quantum ad hoc actus rationis non est in potestate nostra, nec imperari potest. Alius autem actus rationis est, dum his quae apprehendit assentit. Si igitur fuerint talia apprehensa, quibus naturaliter intellectus assentiat, sicut prima principia, assensus talium vel dissensus non est in potestate nostra, sed in ordine naturae; et ideo, proprie loquendo, naturae imperio subjacet. Sunt autem quaedam apprehensa, quae non adeo convincunt intellectum, quin possit assentire vel dissentire, vel saltem assensum vel dissensum suspendere propter aliquam causam; et in talibus assensus vel dissensus in potestate nostra est, et sub imperio cadit.

[11] Frequenter animadverti ea quae homines iudicabant ab iis quae intelligebant dissentire (AM V, 52).

B

Aquinas, Descartes thinks that there are some truths which are perceived in such a way as to forced assent; Aquinas calls these first principles, Descartes calls them clear and distinct perceptions. As he wrote to Regius in 1640: our mind is of such a nature that it cannot fail to assent to what is clearly understood.[12] Like Aquinas, Descartes thinks that in other cases the mind is free to assent or dissent; but whereas Aquinas says that assent or dissent in such a case is at the command of the will, Descartes as we have seen regards assent as being, not just commanded by the will but as itself an act of the will. I know of no scholastic prior to Descartes who held this view, and I am unimpressed by the attempts of Gilson and Koyré to find precedent for it in Augustine, Thomas and Scotus.[13]

When he wrote the *Regulae*, Descartes still held the orthodox Thomist view, as we have seen. There is, it is true, one passage which Leslie Beck sees as presupposing the later view 'that judgement whether in its pure or practical use is an assent or dissent, an act of will'.[14] But the passage is most naturally interpreted as applying only to practical matters. Descartes exhorts us, in studying, 'to think solely of increasing the natural light of reason, not with a view to solving this or that scholastic problem but in order that in all the happenings of our life, our intellect may show our will what alternative to choose'.[15] In this passage it is choice, and not judgement, not even practical judgement, which is attributed to the will; though if Descartes had called the choice following deliberation 'judgement' he would not have been departing from scholastic usage.[16] So *pace* Beck, the *Regulae* do

---

[12] Mens nostra est talis naturae, ut non potest clare intellectis non assentiri (AT III, 64).

[13] Koyré quotes a passage from Augustine in which a judgement is attributed to the will; but this concerns the act of faith, and not regular speculative judgement (*Essai dur l'idee de Dieu et les preuves de son existence chez Descartes*, Paris, 1922, p. 78).

Gilson's best text for the assimilation between St. Thomas and Descartes is the following:

Conclusio syllogismi quae fit in operabilibus ad rationem pertinet, et dicitur sententia vel iudicium, quam sequitur electio; et ob hoc ipsa conclusio pertinere videtur ad electionem tanquam ad consequens.

This is far from Descartes' identification of judgement and election; and in any case applies only to practical reasoning (in operabilibus) (S. Th. Ia IIae, 13 1 ad 2).

[14] L. J. Beck, *The Method of Descartes* (Oxford, 1952), p. 17.

[15] Cogitet tantum de naturali rationis lumine augendo, non ut hanc aut illam scholae difficultatem resolvat, sed ut in singulis vitae casibus intellectus voluntati praemonstret quid sit eligendum.

[16] Iudicium est quasi conclusio et determinatio consilii. Determinatur autem consilium primo quidem per sententiam rationis, et secundo per acceptationem appetitus . . . et hoc modo ipsa electio dicitur quoddam iudicium a quo nominatur liberum arbitrium S. Th. I, 84 3 ad. 2.

not differ from the Thomist doctrine that judgement is an act of the intellect.

Some time, then, between 1628 and 1640 Descartes changed his mind about the nature of judgement. It is not easy to discover when or why he did so. The *Discourse on Method* is not helpful: it hardly mentions the will. In the Third Section, while urging the importance of following men's practice rather than their preaching, Descartes observes that many people do not know what they really believe. 'For the mental act of believing a thing is different from the act of knowing that one believes it; and the one act often occurs without the other.'[17] In his commentary Gilson cites here a passage from Regis: 'According to Descartes, the mental act by which we judge something to be good or bad is a function of the will, and the action by which we know that we have judged thus is a function of the intellect. It is no wonder if two functions, one of the intellect and one of the will, are different and can occur apart.'[18] Regis' annotation shows that what is here said is coherent with Descartes' mature theory of judgement; but it does not establish that he already held it. First of all, the passage concerns practical and not speculative judgement; secondly, even someone who thinks that both belief and the knowledge that one believes are acts of the intellect can think it possible for one of them to occur without the other.[19]

We may turn next to Descartes' unpublished writings for a clue in this matter. In 1630 in letters to Mersenne Descartes put forward his famous doctrine of the creation of the eternal truths. It was the common scholastic doctrine that the truths of logic and mathematics were necessary in such a way that not even God could change them: they were not altogether independent of him, because they depended for their truth upon his essence or nature; but they did not depend on his free will in the way that the

[17] L'action de la pensée par laquelle on croit une chose, étant differente de celle par laquelle on connait qu'on la croit, elles sont souvent l'une sans l'autre (AT VI, 23).

[18] Exactement commenté par Pierre-Silvain Regis: 'Car il faut savoir que, selon M. Descartes, l'action de l'esprit par laquelle nous jugeons qu'une chose est bonne ou mauvaise est une fonction qui appartient à la volonté, et que l'action par laquelle nous connaissons que nous avons jugé ainsi est une fonction qui appartient à l'entendement. Ou, ce n'est pas une grande merveille que deux fonctions, dont l'une appartienent à l'entendement et l'autre à la volonté soient differentes, et que l'une puisse être sans l'autre.' Gilson, op. cit., p. 238.

[19] The difficulty is to reconcile what Descartes says here with *Passions*, article I, 19. See the remarks of Professor R. M. McRae in this volume, pp. 61, 68.

existence of the world did. Descartes argued that the scholastics talked of God 'as if he were Jupiter or Saturn, subject to Styx and Fate': in contrast he insisted that it is God who has established these laws in nature just as a King establishes laws in his kingdom. The eternal truths 'are true or possible because God knows them as true or possible; they are not, contrariwise, known to God as true as though they were true independently of him . . . in God knowing and willing are but one thing; so that from the very fact of his willing something he knows it, and for this reason alone is such a thing true'.[20]

Attempts have been made to find sources for this doctrine in Scotus and Ockham; like the attempts to find scholastic precedents for the theory of judgement, they are unconvincing.[21] Both the doctrine of the creation of eternal truths and the theory that judgement is an act of the will are, of course, examples of a 'voluntarist' tendency—a tendency to attribute to the will (human or divine) things which might be attributed to something else (the intellect, or the nature); and such a tendency is to be found in Scotus and Ockham (the happiness of the blessed resides primarily in the will; good and evil are as they are because God so wills). But the resemblance seems to end there. And the connection, if there is one, between the two Cartesian doctrines, is fairly tenuous. It is true that if in God knowing and willing two and three to make five is one and the same act, then we have an act which can be regarded as at the same time an act of the intellect and of the will. But that this is the case with God, whose nature is simple and undivided, does not tell us anything about what is the case in man where intellect and will are distinct. Descartes does not even use the word 'judgement' about God in this context, though no doubt if he did, he would say that in God judging, just like willing and creating, was identical with seeing, knowing or understanding.

Mersenne informed Descartes that his doctrine resembled that of the Oratorian P. Gibieuf, who published in 1630 his *De Libertate Dei et Hominis*. Descartes, on receiving the book from Mersenne

[20] Sunt tantum verae aut possibiles quia Deus illas veras aut possibiles cognoscit, non autem contra veras a Deo cognosci quasi independenter ab illo sint verae . . . en Dieu ce n'est qu'un de vouloir et de connaître; de sorte que ex hoc ipso quod aliquid velit, ideo cognoscit, et ideo tantum talis res est vera (AT I, 149).
[21] There is no real evidence for Koyré's view that Descartes read Scotus in the 1620's. Even according to Koyré, Scotus held only that God could change moral laws such as the decalogue, not logical or mathematical truths.

(cf AT I, 153, 174, 220) had pleasure, as Baillet says, to find wherewithal to authorize what he conceived of indifference and freewill. But though Gibieuf's views on the liberty of God, and on the Jesuit doctrine of liberty of indifference, were very close to those of Descartes, there is nothing in his *De Libertate* to suggest that speculative judgement is an act of the will. On the contrary, the book reaffirms the traditional doctrine on this point. 'It is to be observed that liberty is an appetitive, not a cognitive faculty; because it is a faculty whose object is the end or the supreme good, which is an object of appetite not of intellect. It is no objection to this that it is called the faculty of free decision or judgement, and that judgement or decision is an act of reason. For it is called the faculty of free decision, both because it is moved by the free decision or judgment, and because free decision or judgment, when it is perfect and, as they say, practico-practical, includes its acceptance; not that its actual act is a Judgement or decision.'[22]

Altogether, I can find no passage in Descartes' letters prior to the writing of the *Meditations* which clearly teaches that judgement is an act of the will. This makes it the more surprising that when it is put forward there it is not presented as a novel thesis which needs to be argued for, but is presupposed and applied before being stated in so many words. Only Gassendi seems to have objected, and that not in his first objections, but in his Instances, of which one is thus summarised: 'To avoid confusion the intellect and the will should be so distinguished that whatever concerns cognition and judgement should be attributed to the intellect, and whatever concerns appetition and choice should be attributed to the will.'[23]

Being unable to find a historical source from which Descartes might have borrowed the doctrine that judgement is an act of the will, we must ask what philosophical considerations may have led him to devise it for himself. The one which first suggests itself is

---

[22] Observandum secundo, libertatem esse facultatem appetitivam, non cognoscitivam: quia est facultas cuius objectum est finis, sive summum bonum, quod est appetitus non intellectus. Nec refert quod vocetur facultas liberi arbitrii sive iudicii, iudicium autem sive arbitrium sit actus rationis. Vocatur enim facultas liberi arbitrii, tum quia movetur a libero arbitrio sive iudicio, tum quia liberum arbitrium sive iudicium (quando perfectum est et practice practicum, ut vocant) eius iam acceptationem includit; non autem quod actus eius elicitus sit iudicium ipsum sive arbitrium (op. cit., 355).

[23] Vitandae confusionis gratia debere intellectum et voluntatem ita distingui ut quicquid cognitionis et judicii est, ad intellcetum pertineat; quicquid appetitionis electionisque, ad voluntatem (AT VII, 404).

the fact that judgement, even speculative judgement, is, often at least, a voluntary matter. What we believe is influenced by our desires; rash judgement or stubborn incredulity is blamed as a moral fault; courage and effort may be required to retain rational conviction in face of emotional pressures. In the controversy with Regius there is some evidence that this consideration was the origin of Descartes theory. In the *Notes on a Programme*, Descartes objects to Regius' dividing understanding into perception and judgement. 'I however saw that, over and above perception, which is required in order that we may judge, there must needs be affirmation or negation to constitute the form of judgement, and that it is often possible for us to withhold our assent, even if we perceive a thing. I attributed the act of judging, which consists solely in assent, that is in affirmation or negation, not to the perception of the understanding, but to the determination of the will.'[24]

In his doctoral thesis, *La doctrine Cartesienne de la liberté*, Etienne Gilson argued, on the basis of this and other texts, that the origin of Descartes' theory of judgement was to be sought in his desire to adapt Aquinas' theodicy to his own purposes. The problem of evil presented itself to Descartes above all as the problem of error. There existed a set of arguments in Aquinas to show how God could be exonerated from blame for human sin. By making judgement an act of the will, Descartes assimilated erroneous judgement to sinful volition. Thus he was able to use Aquinas' arguments to exonerate the author of nature from blame for human fallibility. 'The problem of sin is the theological form of the problem of error and the problem of error is the philosophical form of the problem of sin.'[25]

Two objections may be made to Gilson's thesis, one sound and the other unsound. The unsound objection runs as follows. It is just not the case that all judgement is voluntary in the sense of being avoidable. There are many judgements, as Descartes is the

---

[24] Ego enim, cum viderem, praeter perceptionem, quae praerequiritur ut iudicemus, opus esse affirmatione vel negatione ad formam iudicii constituendam, nobisque saepe liberum esse ut cohibeamus assensionem, etiamsi rem percipiamus: ipsum actum iudicandi, qui non nisi in assensu, hoc est, in affirmatione vel negatione consistit, non retuli ad perceptionem intellectus, sed ad determinationem voluntatis (AT VIIIa 363).

[25] 'La problème du péché est la forme théologique de celui de l'erreur et la problème de l'erreur est las forme philosophique de celui de la péché (op. cit., p. 284).

first to admit, that we cannot help making. Even the *Notes on a Programme* merely say 'nobis *saepe* liberum esse ut cohibeamus assensionem', and it appears disingenuous for Gibson to paraphrase this, as he does, 'nous savons par expérience que cette affirmation et cette négation sont *toujours* en notre pouvoir' (op. cit., p. 276).

This objection is unsound because Descartes does not consider it necessary for a judgement to be voluntary that it should be avoidable. Like most scholastics, Descartes was willing to call an act voluntary if it was in accordance with the agent's desires, whether or not it was avoidable; indeed, unlike most scholastics, he was prepared to call an unavoidable, but welcome, action 'free' as well as 'voluntary' (AT IV, 116).[26] Moreover, it is undoubtedly true, as Gilson says, that in the Fourth Meditation Descartes does use in the interest of theodicy arguments very parallel to those of Aquinas.

The crucial objection to Gilson's thesis is that it was not necessary, for Descartes to be able to exploit Aquinas' arguments, that he should have made judgement an act of the will; it was sufficient for him to make it a voluntary act of the intellect. In scholastic terminology, he did not need to regard judgement as an *actus elicitus voluntatis*; it was perfectly sufficient for him to regard it, as Aquinas himself did, as an *actus imperatus a voluntate*.[27] Not all voluntary acts are acts of the will: walking, for instance, may be a voluntary act but it is an act of the body rather than of the will. Descartes might reject this example because, as he says often, nothing is completely in my power but my thoughts (e.g. *Discourse*, Part III; letter 154). But imagination, and intellectual thought are under the control of will—we can decide what we are going to think about—but are not acts of the will. 'Our desires are of two sorts: one of which consists in the actions of the soul which terminate in the soul itself, as when we desire to love God, or generally speaking, apply our thoughts to some object which is not material. . . . When our soul applies itself to imagine something which does not exist, as when it represents to itself an enchanted

[26] Moreover any erroneous judgement was for Descartes voluntary in the sense of avoidable.

[27] Descartes does not, so far as I know, use the pair *actus elicitus actus imperatus*. But he frequently uses the terminology of eliciting acts (e.g. *Med.* IV, AT VII, 60; N. in P, AT VIIIa, 363) and the terminology of *actus imperatus* is implied in the letter 463.

palace or a chimera, and also when it applies itself to consider something which is only intelligible and not imaginable, e.g. to consider its own nature, the perceptions which it has of these things depend principally on the act of will which causes it to perceive them.' Such perceptions, then are voluntary; but they are perceptions of the intellect, not inclinations of the will (*Passions*, articles 18, 20). The problem we might say is not that error belongs to philosophy and sin to theology; it is that the object of the intellect is truth, and that of the will is goodness; that error is a matter of falsehood, and sin of badness. And this problem Gilson's theory is impotent to solve.

Put in less scholastic terms, the problem is why, and with what justification, Descartes should lump judgement together with desire and aversion and separate it from perception and imagination. One reason might be that judgement and desire are, on Descartes' theory, the only acts which we perform if and only if we want to perform them. Walking is something which we do only if we want to; but not every time we want to walk do we succeed in walking. If we want to imagine something, on the other hand, we succeed in doing so; but we often have thoughts in our imagination which we do not will to be there. Neither of walking nor imagination, therefore, is it true that they are acts which we perform if and only if we want to. Judgement and desire, of which this is true, are therefore voluntary in a special way.

But there is a further reason for regarding judgement as an act of the will: and light may be thrown on this from an unexpected quarter. In modern times Frege has taught us to make a sharp distinction between the sense of a sentence which remains the same whether a sentence appears as a complete unit of communication or as a hypothetical clause in a longer sentence, and the assertion of a sentence which he marked by a special sign whose function was to indicate that the reference or truth-value of what follows it is 'the true'.[28] Many other writers have followed Frege, notably R. M. Hare, who in *The Language of Morals* made a distinction in sentences between a *phrastic* (which contains the descriptive content of the sentence) and a *neustic* (which marks the mood of a sentence, and of which Frege's assertion sign would be

---

[28] *The Philosophical Writings of Gottlob Frege*, ed. Geach and Black (Oxford, 1952), pp. 62ff.

an example).[29] The two sentences 'You will shut the door' and
'You, shut the door' have something in common—the state of
affairs which would verify the prediction is the same as the state of
affairs which would constitute obedience to the command, namely
your shutting the door. But as sentences in different moods they
differ; and the similarity and differences might be brought out by
rephrasing them

> Your shutting the door in the immediate future, please
> Your shutting the door in the immediate future, yes.

It is not difficult to see a similarity between Descartes' theory
of judgement and the theory of Frege and Hare. The perceptions
of the intellect, it might be said, are concerned with the unasserted
phrastics; an affirmative judgement is as it were the mental attachment of the neustic 'yes' to the phrastic presented by the intellect,
the mental attachment of the assertion sign to the Fregean 'sense'
which is the object of perception. There is of course the difference
that neither Frege nor Hare has a negative neustic; negation is
regarded not as the polar opposite of assertion, but as the assertion
of a phrastic with a negative sense, containing within itself the
logical constant for negation.

In two passages Descartes seems to make the contrast between
phrastic and neustic in the scholastic terminology of matter and
form. In the Third Meditation, having said that only those of his
thoughts that are like pictures really deserve the name of 'idea', he
goes on to say 'Other thoughts have other forms in addition: when
I will, am afraid, assert, or deny, there is always something which
I take as the subject of my thought; but my thought comprises
more than the likeness of the thing in question; of these some are
termed volitions or emotions, others are termed judgements'.[30]
The word 'subjectum' suggests to a modern reader the translation
'topic'; but in fact it is used in scholastic terminology as a synonym

---

[29] *The Language of Morals* (Oxford, 1952), pp. 18ff. In his more recent work
Hare distinguishes what he called a neustic into neustic, tropic and elistic.
These refinements are not necessary for a comparison with Descartes, who
does not make any analogous distinctions.

[30] Aliae vero alias quaedam praeterea formas habent; ut cum volo, cum
timeo, cum affirmo, cum nego, semper quidem aliquam rem ut subjectum meae
cogitationis apprehendo, sed aliquid etiam amplius quam istius rei similitudinem
cogitatione complector; et ex his aliae voluntates, sive affectus, aliae autem
iudicia appellantur (AT VII, 37).

for 'materia' in contrast to 'forma', which is explicitly used to refer to what differentiates a judgement from a pure idea.[31]

In this passage judgements are contrasted with volitions rather than classified as a species of volition; this makes clear that Descartes uses 'volition' in a narrow sense as well as a broad sense, volitions strictly so called being a species of a genus of acts of will which includes also judgements.[32] In the other passage which uses scholastic terminology we are told very explicitly that judgement is an act of the will. This is in the passage already quoted from the *Notes on a Programme*, where Descartes is objecting to Regius' classification of mental phenomena. 'Then he divides what he calls the intellect into perception and judgement, which does not accord with my view. I observed that besides the perception which was required for judgement there must also be an affirmation or negation to constitute the form of judgement; and that it is often open to us to withhold our assent even if we perceive a thing. And so I attributed the act of judging, which consists purely in assent, i.e. affirmation and negation, not to the perception of the intellect, but to the determination of the will' (AT VIII 303).

The statement that the intellect is concerned with the un-asserted phrastics needs some qualification; for Descartes uses 'intellect' no less than 'will' in two senses. In one sense the intellect is the possession of the power to recall and combine ideas; it is in this sense that every judgement presupposes an act of the intellect, since judgements must concern ideas, neustics must be attached to phrastics. In another sense the intellect is the faculty which produces clear and distinct ideas and intuits their truth; it is in this sense that Descartes can explain error by saying that the faculty of judging extends farther than the faculty of understanding. He explained this to Gassendi in the Fifth

[31] Cf. also II replies: distinguendum est inter materiam sive rem ipsam cui assentimur, et rationem formalem quae movet voluntatem ad assentiendum.

[32] On the basis of this passage Brentano argued that Descartes did not really regard judgement as an act of the will at all; he explains away Principle 32 and the *Notes on a Programme* by saying that Descartes means judgement is an *actus imperatus voluntatis* and not an *actus elicitus voluntatis*. He does not seem to have noticed that in the Fourth Meditation Descartes speaks of 'eliciendos illos actus voluntatis, sive illa iudica, in quibus fallor' (AT VII, 60). The French makes even clearer the identity of the act of the will and the judgements: 'Dieu concourt avec moi pour former les actes de cette volonté, c'est à dire les jugements dans lesquels je me trompe' (AT IX, 48). See Brentano, *The True and the Evident* (London, 1966), pp. 28–32.

Replies (AT VII, 376). 'When you judge that the mind is a rarefied body, you can understand that it is a mind, that is, a thinking thing, and you can understand that a rarefied body is an extended thing; but you do not understand that one and the same thing is both thinking and extended; this is something you merely will to believe because you believed it before and you do not like changing your mind. When you judge that an apple, which happens to be poisoned, is suitable food, you understand that its odour and colour etc. are pleasant, but not that it is a good thing for you to eat; but because you want it so, you judge it so. And so I agree that we do not will anything about which we understand nothing at all; but I deny that we understand as much as we will; because we can, about one and the same thing, will much and know very little.'[33]

The ambiguity of Descartes' 'intellectus' can be paralleled in the English word 'understanding' which is the nearest word to Descartes' French 'entendement'. When we use the word 'understanding', like Locke, as a name for a very general faculty, we might say that the belief that eighteen is a prime number is an operation of the understanding; but of course in another sense no-one can understand that eighteen is a prime number since it is not. So, in this passage of the reply to Gassendi, Descartes restricts the verb 'intelligere' to his adversary's correct performances—understanding what mind is, and what body is—and refuses to apply it to his mistaken idea that mind is a kind of body.

There is a difference between phrastics and the 'materia' of Descartes' judgements in that phrastics are unambiguously composite, propositional, containing argument and function; whereas the matter of Cartesian judgement is ideas, and ideas may be simple (e.g. the idea *of* mind) or composite (e.g. the idea 'horse with wings') and composite ideas seem sometimes to be expressed nominally (idea *of* a horse with wings) and sometimes propositionally (idea *that* a horse has wings). Sometimes Descartes writes as

[33] Ita cum iudicas mentem esse tenue quoddam corpus intelligere quidem potes, ipsam esse mentem, hoc est, rem cogitantem, itemque tenue corpus esse rem extensam; unam autem et eandem esse rem quae cogitat et quae sit extensa, profecto non intelligis, sed tantummodo vis credere, quia iam ante credidisti nec libenter de sententia decedis. Ita cum pomum, quod forte venenatum est, iudicas tibi in alimentum convenire, intelligis quidem eius odorem, colorem, et talia grata esse, non autem ideo ipsum pomum tibi esse utile in alimentum; sed quia its vis, ita iudicas. Atque sic fateor quidem nihil nos velle de quo non aliquo modo intelligamus; sed nego noe aeque intelligere et velle; possumus enim de eatem re velle permulta et perpauca tantum cognoscere (AT VII, 377).

if even a non-propositional idea can be asserted; whereas of course it would be impossible to attach a neustic to a name standing alone. In such a case, presumably the assertion amounts to the assertion of an extra-mental existence of the thing represented by the idea.[34]

The work of the intellect in the strict sense involves not only the understanding of ideas but also seeing the combination between ideas (as, that thought is linked with existence). The intellect, in the wide sense, includes the imagination, whose function is to combine together the ideas of various bodily objects (forming, say, the idea of a goat-stag out of the idea of a goat and the idea of a stag). But it is not clear, in Descartes' system, what faculty is responsible for linking together non-corporeal ideas which do not belong together in reality: e.g. what links the ideas together in the idea that mind is a rarefied body? In Gassendi, one might think, it is the will that links these ideas together, just as it is the will which judges the composite idea so formed to be true. But this will not apply in the case of Descartes, whose will makes no such judgement, and who yet in order to reject the judgement has to put the two ideas together in the sentence 'The mind is not a rarefied body.'

The comparison between Descartes' perceptions and Hare's phrastics, then, though illuminating, needs qualification. Let us now turn to the other element, the neustic. Does a consideration of this throw any light on why Descartes considered judgement an act of the will? If the command 'Jones shut the door' can be rewritten 'Shutting of the door by Jones, please', it seems that Jones's acceptance of, or assent to, this command, might be expressed by 'Shutting of the door by Jones, yes'. Elsewhere I have suggested that wishes, desires and other pro-attitudes could be similarly expressed artificially by a unit consisting of a phrastic describing the approved state of affairs, and a neustic indicating the attitude of approval.

Now of course when Jones agrees to the order 'shut the door' by saying 'yes', he means 'yes I will', not 'yes that is the case'. None the less, it is a striking fact that we can give an affirmative response not only to propositions and questions, but also to commands and projects, by the same word 'yes'. Our attitudes to

[34] Cf. Third Meditation, AT VIII, 33; and the letter to Mersenne, no. 308, in which Descartes says that all ideas not involving affirmation or negation are innate.

both assertions and proposals may be described in terms of affirmation and negation; both may be characterised as 'assent' or 'dissent'; both as forms of commitment. Assent to both a proposition and a proposal may be sincere or insincere, rash or cautious, right or wrong.

It is this, I think, which provides the main justification for Descartes' treatment of judgement as an act of the will. For what is it, after all, to ascribe particular actions to one or other faculty? It is to group those actions together in virtue of common features of description and assessment which apply to them. If we take together all those mental activities which can have rightness or wrongness ascribed to them, we will find that they include all those activities which Descartes ascribed to the will and exclude those which he ascribed to the intellect.

But this justification of Descartes' procedure suggests immediately an objection to it. It may be wrong to think that the earth is larger than the sun, and wrong to have vengeful desires; but the wrongness in the one case consists in falsehood and in the other case in evil. The right, we might say grandly, is a genus of which the species are the true and the good; and Descartes' classification emphasizes the unity of the genus at the cost of ignoring the diversity of the species.

It would be open to Descartes to make the following reply. It is indeed the case that judgement, unlike desires, can be classified as true or false. But it is not true that judgements cannot be classified as good and evil. Believing that the human mind, properly used, was infallible, Descartes believed that every erroneous judgement was a moral fault. 'What theologian or philosopher' he asked 'or indeed what rational man has ever denied that we are in less danger of error the more clearly we understand something before assenting to it, and that it is a sin to make a judgement before the case is known?'[35] Moreover, the truth and falsehood which belongs to a judgement, Descartes might have said, belongs to it not in so far as it is an assent, but in so far as what is assented to—what is presented by the intellect—corresponds or does not correspond to reality. Erik Stenius has pointed out that unasserted phrastics possess a truth-value

[35] Quis unquam vel Philosophus vel Theologus, vel tantum homo ratione utens non confessus est eo minori in errandi periculo nos versari, quo clarius aliquid intelligimus, antequam ipsi assentiamur, atque illos peccare qui causa ignota iudicium ferunt (II Replies, AT VII, 147).

independently of being asserted; what is contained in an if-clause,
for example, either is or is not a description of what is the case,
even though, since it occurs in an if-clause, it is not being put
forward as such a description.[36] This is a fact which is presupposed in the truth-tabular definition of the logical constants.
The truth of assertions might be regarded as parasitic on this: an
assertion is true if and only if what is asserted is true, i.e. is a
description which corresponds to reality.

In fact Descartes does not answer along these lines. Instead he
says: 'Ideas considered in themselves and not referred to something else, cannot strictly speaking be false; whether I imagine a
she-goat or a chimera, it is not less true that I imagine the one
rather than the other. Again, falsehood is not to be feared in the
will or the emotions; I may desire what is evil, or what does not
exist anywhere, but it is none the less true that I desire it. Only
judgements remain: it is here that I must take precautions against
falsehood.'[37] This, as I have remarked elsewhere, is a strange
argument.[38] One could as well argue that judgements in themselves could not be false, on the grounds that whether what I judge
is true or false, it is none the less true that I judge. I think this
reveals a genuine confusion in Descartes. His theory of judgement
involves an important insight which he failed to follow up.[39]

The point which Descartes has missed is what we may call—to
adapt an expression of J. L. Austin's—the *onus of match*.[40] If we
express assent to a proposition or a project in the phrastic-neustic
form, each expression will contain a description of a possible state
of affairs, plus an assent-indicator. But let us suppose that the
possible state of affairs does not, at the relevant time, obtain.
Do we fault the assent, or the state of affairs? Do we condemn the
original assent as a false assertion, or do we complain about the

<hr />

[36] *Wittgenstein's 'Tractatus'* (Ithaca, N.Y., 1960), p. 165ff.

[37] Quad ad ideas attinet, si solae in se spectentur, nec ad aliud quid illas
referam, falsae proprie esse non possunt; nam sive capram, sive chimaeram
imaginer, non minus verum est me unam imaginari quam alteram. Nulla etiam
in ipsa voluntate, vel affectibus, falsitas est timenda; nam quamvis prava,
quamvis etiam ea quae nusquam sunt, possim optare, non tamen ideo non verum
est illa me optare. Ac proinde sola supersunt iudicia, in quibus mihi cavendum
set ne fallar (AT VII, 37).

[38] *Descartes* (New York, 1968), p. 117.

[39] A further example of the same confusion occurs in the reply to Gassendi:
Cum autem prave iudicamus, non ideo prave volumus, sed forte pravum quid;
nec quidquam prave intelligimus, sed tantum dicimur prave intelligere, quando
iudicamus nos aliquid amplius intelligere quam revera intelligamus (AT VII,
377).

[40] 'How to Talk', *Philosophical Papers*, p. 190.

subsequent state of affairs as an unsatisfactory outcome? Elsewhere, I have tried to clarify this point by considering the different relation of an architect's plan, and a plan in a guidebook, to a building. 'If the building and the plan do not agree, then if the plan is in a guidebook, it is the plan which is wrong; if the plan was made by an architect, then there is a mistake in the building.'[41] In the relation between the guidebook and the building, the onus of match is on the plan; in the relation between the architectural drawing and the building, the onus of match is on the building. So, in general, in assenting to a proposition, we place an onus on a phrastic to match the world; in assenting to a command or project we place an onus on something non-linguistic (primarily, our own actions) to match a phrastic.

Descartes, in lumping together affirmation and desire, negation and aversion, confounds the different onus of match involved in the two different kinds of assent and dissent. This, it seems to me, is the fundamental defect in his theory of judgement as an act of the will. The absence of the notion of onus of match at this point is the more surprising as a very similar notion plays a fundamental part in Descartes' moral theory. 'My third maxim was to try always to conquer myself rather than fortune; to change my desires rather than the order of the world' (*Discourse*, part 3).

II. *The Evolution of Descartes' Doctrine of Freedom*

Throughout the history of philosophy there have been two contrasting methods of expounding the nature of human freewill. The first is in terms of power: we are free in doing something if and only if it is in our power not to do it. The second is in terms of wanting: we are free in doing something if and only if we do it because we want to do it. This is the distinction which Hume made when he urged us to distinguish 'betwixt the liberty of spontaneity, as it is call'd in the schools, and the liberty of indifference; betwixt that which is oppos'd to violence, and that which means a negation of necessity and causes' (*Treatise*, III, II, II). Liberty defined in terms of wanting is liberty of spontaneity; liberty defined in terms of power is liberty of indifference. As Hume observed, the former, but not the latter, is compatible with causal determinism.

[41] 'Practical Inference', *Analysis* 26.3.68. The point was first made by Miss Anscombe (*Intention*, p. 56), who modestly but incorrectly attributes it to Theophrastus.

In their accounts of human freedom most philosophers have combined both elements and Descartes is no exception. In the Fourth Meditation we read 'Freewill consists simply in the fact that we are able alike to do and not to do a given thing (that is, can either assert or deny, either seek or shun); or rather, simply in the fact that our impulse towards what our intellect presents to us as worthy of assertion or denial, as a thing to be sought or shunned, is such that we feel ourselves not to be determined by any external force'.[42] This appears tantamount to saying 'Freewill consists in liberty of indifference, or rather in liberty of spontaneity'. One immediately wants to ask: what is the force of the 'or rather' here? Does it mark second thoughts, so that Descartes is withdrawing the statement that freewill consists in liberty of indifference and replacing it with the more correct statement that it consists in liberty of spontaneity? Or does it mean that liberty of indifference, properly understood, is identical with liberty of spontaneity so that the *'vel potius'* means something like 'or, in other words'? The answer, I think, is not quite either of these: it is rather that Descartes thinks that freewill often does consist in liberty of indifference, but that sometimes it consists only in liberty of spontaneity, and that is all that is essential to it. He goes on: 'There is no need for me to be impelled both ways in order to be free; on the contrary, the more I am inclined one way—either because I clearly understand it under the aspect of truth and goodness, or because God has so disposed my inmost consciousness— the more freely do I choose that way.'[43] In this passage there is a difficulty in the translation of the phrase 'in utramque partem ferri posse'. If this is taken to mean 'there is no need for me to be able to go both ways'—i.e. to *act* either way—then the sentence contains an outright denial that liberty of indifference is necessary for freewill. Geach, however, takes the passive sense of *ferri* seriously, and translates 'there is no need for me to be impelled both ways'—i.e. to have reasons on both sides. Taken this way,

[42] Voluntas, sive arbitrii libertas, . . . tantum in eo consistit quod idem vel facere vel non facere—hoc est affirmare vel negare, prosequi vel fugere—possimus, vel potius in eo tantum quod ad id quod nobis ab intellectu proponitur affirmandum vel negandum, sive prosequendum vel fugiendum, ita feramur, ut a nulla vi externa nos ad id determinari sentiamus (AT VII, 57).
[43] Neque enim opus est me in utramque partem ferri posse, ut sim liber, sed contra, quo magis in unam propendeo, sive quia rationem veri et boni in ea evidenter intelligo, sive quia Deus intima cogitationis meae its disponit, tanto liberius illam eligo.

the sentence is not incompatible with the view that liberty of
indifference is essential to genuine freedom; for a full-blooded
liberty of indifference would be a freedom to act either way even
though the reasons for acting might be all on one side.

I think that Geach's rendering is correct: it is borne out by
the French version of the Duc de Luynes which, we are told, was
revised by Descartes himself. This reads 'Il n'est pas nécessaire
que je sois indifférent à choisir l'un ou l'autre des deux contraires'.
At first sight this too looks like a denial of the need for liberty of
indifference: but in fact when Descartes uses the word 'indifference' he does not mean what Hume and the scholastics meant by
indifference. This point is made explicitly in the correspondence
with Mesland which we shall consider later; but it is clear enough
from what follows in the *Meditations*. 'The indifference that I am
aware of when there is no reason urging me one way rather than
the other, is the lowest grade of liberty.'[44] But the indifference
which is the balance of reasons is not the indifference which is the
ability to act either way. The present text does not by itself tell us
whether Descartes believed such an ability to remain when all the
reasons are on one side. 'If I always saw clearly what is good and
true, I should never deliberate as to what I ought to judge or
choose; and thus, although entirely free, I could never be indifferent.'[45] The fact that I would not have to deliberate ('je ne serais
jamais en peine de déliberer' as the French has it) if I always saw
what was good does not establish that I would always *do* what was
good. So the indifference which is here said to be inessential to
freedom is the indifference which consists in the balancing of
reasons and not the indifference which is the ability to act either
way.

However, shortly afterwards, in the case of the *cogito* Descartes
expressly denies that such an ability exists. 'I could not but judge
to be true what I understood so clearly; not because I was com-
pelled to do so by any external cause, but because the great
illumination of my understanding was followed by a great inclination of the will; and my belief was the more free and spontaneous

[44] Indifferentia illa, quam experior cum nulla me ratio in unam partem magis
quam in alteram impellit, est infimus gradus libertatis.
[45] At VII, 58: si semper quid verum et bonum sit clare viderem, nunquam de
eo quod esset iudicandum vel eligendum deliberarem; atque ita, quamvis plane
liber, nunquam tamen indifferens esse possum.

C

for my not being indifferent in the matter.'[46] A truth so clearly
seen, then, cannot but be judged to be the case; so the ability not
to judge, which in this case would constitute liberty of indifference,
is lacking. Where there is no such clarity, however, indifference
remains and this is true not only where there are no reasons, or
equal reasons, on either side, but wherever the reasons on one side
fall short of certainty. For the thought of their uncertainty itself
constitutes a reason on the other side. 'However much I may be
drawn one way by probable conjectures, the mere knowledge that
they are only conjectures and not certain and indubitable reasons
is enough to incline my assent the other.'[47] God, we are told, has
'given me the liberty to assent or not to assent to things of which
he put no clear and distinct perception in my understanding'.[48]

The Fifth Meditation and the Second Replies make clear that
God has given me no such liberty in cases where I do have clear
and distinct perception. 'There are some things which are so
clear and simple that we cannot think of them without believing
them to be true.'[49] The Seventh Axiom, quoted earlier, says 'The
will of a thinking thing is impelled, voluntarily of course and freely,
since this is of the essence of the will, but none the less infallibly,
towards a good clearly known to it'.[50]

The *Principles* repeats and expands the doctrine of the
Meditations. But when freewill is first mentioned in Principle 37 it
looks as if Descartes is attributing liberty of indifference to the
assent of clear truths. He writes: 'It is a supreme perfection in man
to act voluntarily or freely, and thus to be in a special sense the
author of his own actions, and to deserve praise for them. . . . It
is more to our credit that we embrace the truth when we do,
because we do this freely, than it would be if we could not but

---

[46] Non potui quidem non iudicare illud quod tam clare intelligebam verum
esse; non quod ab aliqua vi externa fuerim ad id coactus, sed quia ex magna
luce in intellectu magna consequuta est propensio in voluntate, atque ita tanto
magis sponte et libere illud credidi, quanto minus fui ad istud ipsum indifferens
(AT VII, 59).
[47] Quantumvis enim probabiles conjecturae me trahant in unam partem, sola
cognita quod sint tantum conjecturae, non autem certae atque indubitabiles
rationes, sufficit ad assensionem meam in contrarium impellendam.
[48] Mihi libertatem dederit assentiendi vel non assentiendi quibusdam,
quorum claram et distinctam perceptionem in intellectu meo non posuit (AT
VII, 61).
[49] Quaedam sunt tam perspicua, simulque tam simplicia, ut nunquam
possimus de iis cogitare, quin vera esse credamus (AT VII, 145).
[50] Rei cogitantis voluntas fertur, voluntarie quidem et libere, hoc enim est de
essentia voluntatis, sed nihilominus infallibiliter, in bonum sibi clare cognitum
(AT VII, 166).

embrace it.'⁵¹ He goes on to say that in *many* cases 'we have power
to assent or not assent at our pleasure'.⁵² During the exercise of
Cartesian doubt 'we were conscious of freedom to abstain from
believing what was not quite certain and thoroughly examined'.⁵³

However, this freedom does not hold in all cases, as soon
transpires. It does not extend to things which *are* certain and
examined: because there were some things which even to a
Cartesian doubter were beyond doubt.

The impossibility of withholding assent from clearly perceived
truths is explicitly reasserted in Principle 43. This (principle) is
imprinted by nature on the minds of all in such a way that as
often as we perceive something clearly, we spontaneously assent to
it, and we cannot in any way doubt that it is true.⁵⁴ Despite a
superficial impression, therefore, there is no difference of doctrine
between the *Meditations* and the *Principles*.

The *Principles* were published in 1644. On the 2nd of May of
the same year, Descartes wrote to the Jesuit Denis Mesland, then
in his final year as a theology undergraduate at La Flèche, a letter
which contains his fullest treatment of the problem of freewill.
The most important part of the letter is a commentary on the
passage from the *Meditations* '*ex magna luce in intellectu sequintur
magna propensio in voluntate*'. Descartes agrees with Mesland that
one can suspend one's judgement; but only by distracting one's
attention; one cannot refrain from desiring a good clearly seen
to be good. 'If we see very clearly that something is good for us
it is very difficult—and on my view impossible, as long as one
continues in the same thought—to stop the course of our desire.
But the nature of the soul is such that it does not attend for more
than a moment to a single thing; and so as soon as our attention

⁵¹ Summa quaedam in homine perfectio est quod agat per voluntatem, hoc
est libere, atque its peculiari quodam modo sit author suarum actionum, et ob
ipsas laudem mereatur. . . . Magis profecto nobis tribuendum est, quod verum
amplectamur, cum amplectimur, quia voluntarie id agimus, quam si non
possemus non amplecti (AT VIII, 19). At first sight this appears to mean that
when we embrace truth clearly seen we are free not to embrace it; but from the
sequel it is clear that this is not so. Perhaps Descartes means that in such a case
the credit goes not to us but to the author of our nature, as the credit for the
precise operation of a machine goes to its maker.
⁵² Multis ad arbitrium vel assentiri vel non assentiri possumus.
⁵³ Hanc in nobis libertatem esse experiebamur, ut possemus ab iis credendis
abstinere, quae non plane certa erant et explorata.
⁵⁴ Ita omnium animis a natura impressum est, ut quoties aliquid clare
percipimus, ei sponte assentiamus, et nullo modo possimus dubitare quin sit
verum (AT VIII, 21).

turns from the reasons which make us know that a thing is good
for us, we can call up before our mind some other reason to make us
doubt of it, and so suspend our judgement, or perhaps even make
a contrary judgement.'[55] This is in perfect accord with the
Meditations theory; indeed it is simply an application to the will's
function of pursuing the good of a principle explicitly stated in the
Fifth Meditation, and more clearly in the Second Replies, about
the will's other function of judging the truth. 'I am indeed so
constituted that I cannot but believe something to be true at the
time of perceiving it clearly and distinctly. But I am likewise so
constituted that I cannot fix my mind's eye constantly on the same
object so as to perceive it clearly; and the memory of a previous
judgement often comes back to me when I am no longer attending
to my arguments for having made it. Consequently, other arguments might now be adduced which would readily upset my view
if I had no knowledge of God.'[56]

In the *Meditations* Descartes did not explain how the will falls
into sin as explicitly as he explained how the will falls into error.
This, he told Mesland, was because he wanted to stay within the
limits of natural philosophy and not to involve himself in theological controversies. In this private letter, he is willing to be
explicit. 'If we saw clearly (that what we are doing is evil) it
would be impossible to sin as long as we saw it in that fashion;
that is why they say that whoever sins does so in ignorance.'[57]
This was no novelty, but something which he had said in private
as early as 24 April, 1637. Defending against Mersenne the statement in the *Discourse* that in order to do well it was sufficient to

---

[55] Voyant très clairement qu'une chose nous est propre, il est très mal aisé,
et même, comme je crois, impossible, pendant qu'on demeure en cette pensée,
d'arrêter le cours de notre désir. Mais, parce que la nature de l'âme est de
n'être quasi qu'un moment attentive à une même chose, sitôt que notre attention
se détourne des raisons qui nous font connaître que cette chose nous est propre,
et que nous retenons seulement en notre mémoire qu'elle nous a paru désirable,
nous pouvons représenter à notre esprit quelque autre raison qui nous en fasse
douter, et ainsi suspendre notre jugement, et même aussi peut-être en former un
contraire (AM VI, 144).

[56] Etsi enim eius sim naturae ut, quamdiu aliquid valde clare et distincte
percipio, non possim non credere verum esse, quia tamen eius etiam sum
naturae ut non possim obtutum mentis in eandem rem semper defigere ad illam
clare percipiendam, recurratque saepe memoria iudicii ante facti, cum non
amplius attendo ad rationes propter quas tale quid iudicavi, rationes aliae
possunt quae me, si Deum ignorarem, facile ab opinione deiicerent (AT VII,
69).

[57] Si nous le voyions clairement, il nous serait impossible de pécher, pendant
le temps que nous le verrions en cetter sorte; c'est pourquoi on dit que *omnis
peccans est ignorans* (AM VI, 145).

judge well Descartes had adopted a familiar scholastic viewpoint. 'The will does not tend towards evil except in so far as it is presented to it by the intellect under some aspect of goodness— that is why they say that everyone who sins does so in ignorance. So that if the intellect never presented anything to the will as good without its actually being so, the will could never go wrong in its choice. But the intellect often presents different things to the will at the same time.'[58] This passage clearly implies that the will cannot go against the intellect unless the intellect itself is somehow on both sides of the fence at the same time. In such a case, of course, the perception of the intellect would be confused rather than clear and distinct; and so once again we can draw the conclusion that the will cannot resist the clear and distinct perceptions of the intellect.

In the letter to Mesland Descartes ventures so far into theology as to discuss the merits of Christ. 'A man may earn merit, even though, seeing very clearly what he must do, he does it infallibly and without any indifference, as Jesus Christ did during his earthly life.'[59] How is this to be reconciled with the teaching of the *Principles* that we deserve no praise for what we cannot but do? Descartes explains that the praise is for paying attention. 'Since a man has the power not always to attend perfectly to what he ought to do, it is a good action to pay attention and thus to ensure that our will follows so promptly the light of our understanding that it is in no way indifferent.'[60]. The doctrine then is clear. In the face of clear and distinct perception, freedom to act in a contrary sense is possible only by inattention.

In this letter Descartes makes a comparison between his terminology and that used by the scholastics, especially Jesuit

---

[58] *Voluntas non fertur in malum, nisi quatenus ei sub aliqua ratione boni repraesentatur ab intellectu,* d'où vient ce mot: *omnis peccans est ignorans*; en sorte que si jamais l'entendement ne représentait rien à la volonté comme bien, qui ne le fût, elle ne pourrait manquer en son élection. Mais il lui représente souvent diverses choses en même temps' (AT I, 367). Most commentators seem not to have noticed—and perhaps Descartes himself was not aware—that the dictum he here quotes approvingly *'omnis peccans est ignorans'* is a quotation from his adversary Aristotle (*agnoei oun pas ho mochtheros,* N. Eth. III, 1110b28).

[59] On ne laisse pas de mériter, bien que, voyant très clairement ce qu' il faut faire, on le fasse infailliblement, et sans aucune indifférence, comme a fait Jésus-Christ en cette vie (AM VI, 145).

[60] Car l'homme pouvant n'avoir pas toujours une parfait attention aux choses qu'il doit faire, c'est une bonne action que de l'avoir, et de faire, par son moyen, que notre volonté suive si fort la lumière de notre entendement qu'elle ne soit point du tout indifférente (ibid).

scholastics such as those who taught Mesland. For him, indifference does not mean complete absence of knowledge; but the more
the known reasons balance each other out, the more indifference
there is. 'You regard freedom as not precisely indifference (in
this sense) but rather as a real and positive power to determine
oneself; and so the difference between us is a merely verbal one,
since I agree that the will has such a power. However, I do not see
that it makes any difference to the power whether it is accompanied
by indifference, which you agree is an imperfection, or whether
it is not so accompanied, when there is nothing in the understanding except light, as in the case of the blessed who are confirmed in
grace. And so I call free whatever is voluntary, whereas you wish
to restrict the name to the power to determine oneself only if
accompanied by indifference. But so far as concerns names, I
wish above all to follow usage and precedent.'[61] Indeed, in treating
'voluntary' and 'free' as synonymous, Descartes was following the
precedent of Gibieuf's *De Libertate Dei et Creaturae*. But Gibieuf
was consciously going against the prevailing scholastic tradition
which made a distinction between the two. According to most
scholastics, the saints in heaven loved God voluntarily (because
they did so willingly and not reluctantly) but not freely (since,
clearly seeing the goodness of God, they could not do otherwise).[62]
On this view, everything free was voluntary, but not everything
voluntary was free; and the will, as such, was the capacity for
voluntary action, and so not synonymous with the *free* will or
liberum arbitrium.

Thus far, Descartes' doctrine of liberty is all of a piece. But
there remains one crucial document to consider. This is the letter

[61]Ainsi, puisque vous ne mettez pas la liberté dans l'indifférence précisément,
mais dans une puissance réelle at positive de se déterminer, il n'y a de différence
entre nos opinions que pour le nom; car j'avoue que cette puissance est en la
volonté. Mais, parce que je ne vois point qu'elle soit autre, quand elle est
accompagnée de l'indifférence, laquelle vous avouez être une imperfection, que
quand elle n'en est point accompagnée, et qu'il n'y a rien dans l'entendement
que de la lumière, comme dans celui des bienheureux qui sont confirmés en
grâce, je nomme généralement libre, tout ce qui est volontaire, et vous voulez
restreindre ce nom à la puissance de se déterminer, qui est accompagnée de
l'indifférence. Mais je ne désire rien tant, touchant les noms, que de suivre
l'usage et l'example (AM V, 144).
[62] Op. cit., 56. Voluntati qua natura inest sua libertas . . . Video responderi
posse rationem liberi non esse rationem voluntatis, latiusque patere voluntatem
quam libertatem: quippe voluntatem ad omne bonum se extendere, libertatem
autem ad is tantum quod possit amari vel non amari cum indifferentia . . . sed
si radix libertatis attente consideretur, facile erit non deprehendere solum sed
convincere voluntatem nihil esse nise libertatem.

listed by Adam and Milhaud as being written to Mesland on 9 February 1645; it is number 463 in their collection. M. Alquié, in his *La Découverte Metaphysique de l'Homme chez Descartes*,[63] and in the notes to the Garnier edition of Descartes' works, regards this as marking a decisive break in Descartes' thought. Now at last, in this letter, according to Alquié, Descartes admits that one can reject an evident perception at the moment of perceiving it. 'Il est donc possible, selon Descartes, (contrairement à l'avis de presque tous les commentateurs) de nier l'évidence en presence de l'évidence même de se detourner du bien sous le charme meme de son attrait' (op. cit. 289). Hitherto, it was only by ignorance or inattention that Descartes allowed the possibility of sin or error; in this letter, Alquié believes, Descartes' doctrine 'permet de refuser l'évidence et le bien en connaissance de cause'. Alquié quotes from the letter: 'It is always open to us to hold back from pursuing a clearly known good or from admitting a clearly perceived truth, provided we consider it a good thing to demonstrate the freedom of our will by so doing.' And he concludes 'Il ne s'agit pas, en la lettre de 9 février, de la faiblesse d'une attention se pouvant malaisement fixer sur un object unique, ni de l'élan qui, dans les Méditations, empêchait la conscience de se limiter à des objects finis et la portait vers l'infinie lui-même par un perpétuel dépassement. Ce qui nous détourne du bien, c'est la mauvaise foi que commande l'égoïsme, et sans doute ce désir d'être Dieu qui, dans la Bible, apparaissait déjà comme la source première du péché. Qu'est en effet ce libre arbitre qu'il s'agit d'attester, sinon précisement nous-mêmes?'

No-one, says Alquié, has tried to expound Descartes' doctrine of freedom in this letter 'sans essayer d'en affaiblir le tragique'. I fear I must range myself with the commentators who have been insensitive to the tragedy. I observe first that to base on this letter a theory of an evolution in Descartes' thought is to build on sand. No one knows for certain to whom this letter was written or when. It is given by Clerselier in French as part of a composite letter to Mersenne whose other parts date from 1630 and 1637; but as it alludes to the *Meditations* it must be later than 1640. Adam and Tannery printed it in their third volume in French as a letter to Mersenne with the hypothetical date of May 1641. Alquié says that at this date the letter 'serait incompréhensible, les affirmations

---

[63] 2 ed. (Paris, 1966).

qu'elle contient ne pouvant se situer qu'au terme d'une évolution de pensée comprenant elle-même les Principes et la lettre de 2 mai 1644, contemporaine de leur impression'. But as the only evidence for this evolution is Alquié's interpretation of this very letter, the progress of the evolution cannot be used to date it. Adam and Tannery later found a Latin text of the letter in a MS of the Bibliothèque Mazarine which gave it as a continuation of the letter in French to Mesland of 9 February 1645; accordingly they inserted it in their fifth volume after this letter, and it is retained in this place by Adam and Milhaud in their collection. On internal evidence there seems little doubt that this Latin text is more likely to be the original than the French text given by Clerselier[64]; but the attachment to the letter to Mesland is very dubious. All Descartes' letters to Mesland, as almost always to French-speaking correspondents, are in French, not in Latin. If this fragment belongs to the letter of 9 February, we have a change of language in the middle: why should a letter begun in French end in Latin? Moreover, there is no illusion to the previous letter on freewill to Mesland, though some of the same points are covered. It seems most likely that the compiler of the Bibliothèque Mazarine collection put together letters on transubstantiation and liberty, most but not all of which were to Mesland, rather in the way that Clerselier put together the composite letter to Mersenne from various draft documents he found among Descartes' papers. We must resign ourselves to the fact that we know neither the date nor the destination of this letter.

Whatever the date of the letter, there is in fact no contradiction between its teaching and that of the earlier letter to Mesland. The passage on which M. Alquié builds his theory can easily be explained in accordance with Descartes regular doctrine; and there are other passages which flatly contradict the interpretation put on the letter by Alquié. The letter is so short and so important that I propose at this point to insert a translation of the whole of it.

Descartes (to Mesland) 9 February 1645

As for the freedom of the will, I entirely agree with what the Reverend Father here wrote. Let me explain my opinion more fully. I would like you to notice that 'indifference' seems to me to

---

[64]A note in the Institut copy of Clerselier mentions both that the original of the fragment given by Clerselier is in Latin, and that the date and destination must be considered unknown (AT III, 378).

mean here the state of the will when it is not impelled one way
rather than another by any perception of truth or goodness. This
was the sense in which I took it when I said that the lowest degree
of liberty was that by which we determine ourselves to things to
which we are indifferent. But perhaps others mean by 'indifference' a positive faculty of determining oneself to one or other of
two contraries, that is to say to pursue or avoid, to affirm or deny.
I do not deny that the will has this positive faculty. Indeed, I
think it has it not only with respect to those actions to which it is
not pushed by any evident reasons on one side rather than on the
other, but also with respect to all other actions; so that when a
very evident reason moves us in one direction, although, morally
speaking, we can hardly move in the contrary direction, absolutely
we can. For it is always open to us to hold back from pursuing a
clearly known good, or from admitting a clearly perceived truth,
provided we consider it a good thing to demonstrate the freedom
of our will by so doing.

It must be noted also that liberty can be considered in the
actions of the will before they are elicited, or after they are elicited.

Considered with respect to the time before they are elicited,
it entails indifference in the second sense but not in the first.
Although, when we contrast our own judgement with the com-
mandments of others we say that we are freer to do those things
which have not been prescribed to us by others and in which we
are allowed to follow our own judgement, we cannot similarly
make a contrast within the field of our own judgements and thought
and say that we are freer to do those things which seem neither
good nor evil, or in which there are many reasons pro but as many
reasons contra, than in those in which we see much more good
than evil. For a greater liberty consists either in a greater facility
in determining oneself, or of a greater use of the positive power
which we have of following the worse although we see the better.
If we follow the course which appears to have the most reasons in
its favour, we determine ourselves more easily; if we follow the
opposite, we make more use of that positive power; and thus we
can always act more freely in those cases in which we see much
more good than evil than in those cases which are called *adiaphora*
or indifferent. In this sense too the things which are commanded
us by others, and which we would not otherwise do spontaneously,
we do less freely than the things which are not commanded;
because the judgement that these things are difficult to do is

opposed to the judgement that it is good to do what is commanded; and the more equally these two judgements move us the more indifference, in the first sense, they confer on us.

But liberty considered in the acts of the will at the moment when they are elicited does not entail any indifference either in the first or second sense; because what is done cannot remain undone once it is being done. But it consists simply in ease of operation; and at that point freedom, spontaneity and voluntariness are the same thing. It was in this sense that I wrote that I took a course more freely the more reasons drove me towards it; because it is certain that in that case our will moves itself with greater facility and force.

In the first part of this letter Descartes makes explicit a distinction between two senses of 'indifferent' which was implicit in his 1644 letter when he said that indifference did not imply ignorance, and that wherever there was occasion for sin there was ignorance. When he said that, Descartes clearly did not mean that there could only be sin where the reasons for acting were equally balanced on either side; consequently, he must have meant that there was an indifference which consisted in the possibility of acting against the weight of reason. It is this ability—which we might nickname 'the liberty of perversion'[65]—which Descartes now explicitly distinguishes from indifference in the sense of a balance of reasons. Adding this distinction to the distinction between two kinds of liberty which we saw in the 1644 letter, we get the following table.

Liberty = Voluntas	Liberty of spontaneity	
	Liberty of indifference	Perversion
		Balance

So far the two letters are perfectly compatible. According to Alquié, the two letters differ crucially because according to the 1644 letter we do not enjoy liberty of perversion while we have a clear perception of good whereas in letter number 463 we do so. However, it is perfectly possible to reconcile the two. When Descartes says in letter 463 that it is always open to us to hold back from pursuing a clearly known good, or from admitting a

[65] Potestas . . . sequendi deteriora, quamvis meliora videamus (AM VI, 198).

clearly perceived truth, he need not mean that we can do this at the very moment of perceiving the good and the true. Rather, we must distract our attention, as he said in the 1644 letter. One way of doing this would be to dwell on the thought that it would be a good thing to demonstrate our freewill by perversity. This would provide a reason in the contrary sense, without which the will could not act; and *eo ipso* this would render the perception of truth and goodness unclear; we would, as he said in the 1644 letter, 'merely see confusedly that what we are doing is bad, or remember that we judged it so in the past'. In the 1644 letter he says that we can suspend our judgement 'by representing to our mind some reason to make us doubt of the truth'; letter number 463 suggests a reason one could use.[66]

Alquié sees the possibility of such an interpretation, but says that it would satisfy a merely conceptual demand and would ignore the conflict of our life. But it is possible that Descartes shared a concern for merely conceptual demands; and after all, this is not a minor point in his system. To abandon the theory that clear and distinct perception necessitates the will is to call in question the whole validation of reason in which the *Meditations* culminates. The mark of a clear and distinct idea is that it is one which however much we may exercise our free will we cannot doubt; the only way to find truth is to stick to clear and distinct ideas; the only way to find out which ideas are clear and distinct is to do our damnedest to doubt them and fail to do so. But if clear and distinct ideas can be doubted at the moment they are intuited, we should never have genuine and certain knowledge of anything, we would be back in the morass of doubts of the First Meditation.

The interpretation I have suggested is confirmed by the passage of the letter which immediately follows that on which Alquié rests his case. Descartes distinguishes liberty before the will's act, and liberty during the act. This suggests that we must make a further distinction in the chart we drew, a distinction between simultaneous and subsequent perversion. Thus we have

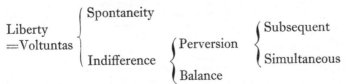

Liberty
=Voltuntas { Spontaneity

Indifference { Perversion { Subsequent / Simultaneous

Balance

---

[66] Without some such reason, doubt would be impossible, as Descartes explained to Gassendi (AT X, 205).

Combining together the data of the two letters, we get the following results. The Blessed in heaven and Christ on earth enjoy liberty of spontaneity, but no liberty of indifference, of any kind, not even the liberty of subsequent perversion. An ordinary man with a clear and distinct idea of what is true and what is good enjoys liberty of spontaneity and liberty of subsequent perversion, but not liberty of simultaneous perversion nor indifference in the sense of balance. An ordinary man with a confused idea of what is true and good enjoys liberty of simultaneous perversion, but only a man who sees no reason to one side rather than another enjoys the full indifference. Such a man, Descartes says, does not enjoy the liberty of spontaneity enjoyed by the others.[67] His argument for this will be considered in a moment.

The final paragraph of the letter 463 is reminiscent of an argument which occurs in Gibieuf's *De Libertate Dei* against the Jesuits who define liberty in terms of an absolute indifference to act or not to act.[68] If that is what liberty consists in, Gibieuf argued, then a man never acts less freely than when he acts freely. For when a man acts, he is not indifferent with regard to acting, but is determined by his very act. To say that it is enough that he could not act when he was on the point of acting, Gibieuf argued, is to say that liberty is only for future acts qua future. On Gibieuf's own view, a man was free if he acted for the sake of the supreme good; and this could be true of him while he was actually acting.[69]

I think that the argument of Gibieuf and Descartes is confused, though it is not easy to explain just where it goes wrong. I do not think, as I once did, that it depends simply on a fallacious inference of modal logic from

[67]	Blessed	C & D	Prob.	Balance
Liberty of Spontaneity	Yes	Yes	Yes	No (Yes)
Liberty of Subs. Perversion	No	Yes	Yes	Yes (No)
Liberty of Simul. Perversion	No.	No	Yes	Yes (No.)
Liberty of Balance	No.	No	No	Yes

[68] This is one of several indications that the Reverend Father mentioned at the beginning of the letter is, as Baillet said, Gibieuf. Another is that the definition of indifference Descartes attributes to the Reverend Father is the one Gibieuf uses, and not the Jesuit one which Mesland accepted and Gibieuf attacked. This suggests that Adam and Tannery's first thoughts on the dating of the letter were perhaps better than their second, since it was in the 30's that we know Descartes was interested in Gibieuf's book.

[69] Quarta probatio ducitur ex contradictione aperta quam includit natura libertatis, ut eam exponere consueverent per indifferentiam absolutam ad agendum et non agendum. Si enim ea sit conditio libertatis, homo nunquam minus libere agit quam cum libere agit. Qui enim agit, non est indifferens ad agendum, sed determinatur actu suo (op. cit. 13; cf. also 165).

It is not possible that both p and not p
to   If p, then it is not possible that not p.

In addition to modality, the argument involves subtle points about tense and action which it would take us too far round to investigate. But the paragraph does contain a point which tells against Alquié. Once one acts, Descartes says, the notions of liberty and spontaneity collapse into each other. This would be altogether untrue on Alquié's view, because in the case of someone with a clear and distinct idea acting with simultaneous perversity, there would be free action, but not spontaneous action; since the man would not be acting with that preponderance of reasons on his side which makes the operation easy and constitutes spontaneity.

Finally I wish to consider the penultimate paragraph of the letter. There is something very dubious about Descartes' argument here to show that indifference of balance is the lowest degree of liberty. He argues that a man enjoys least liberty when the reasons are balanced, because he then enjoys less liberty of spontaneity than when he acts in accord with the greater array of reasons, and less liberty of perversity than when he acts in accord with the lesser array of reasons. He could just as well have argued that a man was most at liberty when the reasons were balanced, since he then enjoys more liberty of perversity than when the majority of reasons are on his side, and more liberty of spontaneity than when the majority of reasons are against him. In fact, having once distinguished liberty of spontaneity from liberty of perversity, Descartes should have said that in the one sense of liberty, action in indifferent matters was freer than action upon clear reasons, and in another sense it was less free. But then he could not have said, what he also wanted to say, that there was a single scale of freedom on which the liberty of indifference occupied the lowest place. This shows that Descartes' theory of freedom will not do as a philosophical account; but it is an incoherence which was present in the theory from the beginning. The doctrine of the *Meditations*, the *Principles* and the letters is all of a piece. I see no reason for thinking that at the age of forty-nine Descartes underwent a spectacular conversion from rationalism to existentialism.

INNATE IDEAS

Robert McRae

Descartes and Leibniz are the two philosophers who are most closely associated today with innate ideas. At the time at which they wrote there was nothing unusual or original in such support. Gilson remarks that Descartes could not fail in 1628 to have encountered innateness all around him, and it is possible to see in Yolton's *Locke and the New Way of Ideas* how general a stir Locke caused when he attacked innate ideas in the *Essay concerning Human Understanding*. What Locke had in mind when he attacked innate ideas was a theory of Ciceronian and Stoic origin, which associated them with universal consent. Locke states it very briefly in this way:

> There is nothing more commonly taken for granted than that there are certain principles, both *speculative* and *practical* (for they speak of both), universally agreed upon by all mankind: which therefore, they argue, must needs be constant impressions which the souls of men receive in their first beings, and which they bring into the world with them, as necessarily and really as they do any of their inherent faculties.[1]

Locke was attacking what he regarded as so widely held a theory that he does not seem to have had any particular philosopher in mind: certainly not Descartes, for what he attacks cannot be attributed to Descartes. The one philosopher he mentions is Lord Herbert of Cherbury, but only as someone whose writings he has consulted after having already stated his case against innate ideas. 'When I had writ this, being informed that my lord *Herbert* had in his books *De Veritate* assigned these innate principles, I presently consulted him, hoping to find, in a man of so great parts, something that might satisfy me in this point and put an end to my enquiry.'[2] Both Descartes and Leibniz dissociated their views from those of Herbert. 'The author [of *De Veritate*], says Descartes, 'takes universal consent for the rule for his truths; while I

---

[1] *An Essay concerning Human Understanding*, I. ii, 2.
[2] Ibid, I, iii, 15.

have the natural light for mine. Mine agrees with his in some respect, for if all men have the same natural light, they ought seemingly all to have the same notions; but it also differs greatly in that there is almost no one who makes good use of this light. Consequently many (for example everyone we know) can consent to the same error, and there are many things which can be known by the natural light, on which no one has yet reflected.'[3] With regard to Herbert, as cited by Locke, Leibniz, in turn, says, 'For myself, I make use of universal consent, not as a principal proof, but as a confirmatory one; for innate truths taken as the *natural light* of reason bear their mark with them as does geometry'.[4]

But if Descartes and Leibniz both dissociate themselves from Herbert's theory of innate ideas, neither has a single alternative theory of innate ideas. There are at least three separate conceptions of innateness in Leibniz. For convenience we can call the first of these the reflective theory of innateness, the second a modified version of *anamnesis*, and the third the dispositional theory of innateness. In the case of Descartes, there is a version of the reflective theory in the third *Meditation*, a modified version of *anamnesis* in the fifth *Meditation*, and in the *Notes against a Programme*, there is what looks like a dispositional theory. Whether it is, is something which must in due course be examined. Finally we must ask whether there is some common ground for the three conceptions of innateness. In the case of Leibniz it may well be that they have no common ground; in the case of Descartes they do.

The Reflective Theory of Innateness

This theory is stated in its clearest form in Leibniz's often quoted comment to Locke in the *New Essays*. 'You oppose to me this axiom received by the philosophers, *that there is nothing in the soul which does not come from the senses.* But you must except the soul itself and its affections. *Nihil est in intellectu quod non fuerit in sensu, excipe: nisi ipse intellectus.* Now the soul comprises being, substance, unity, identity, cause, perception, reason and many other notions which the senses cannot give.'[5] This theory of innateness is far removed from that which maintains that there are

[3] To Mersenne, 16 October, 1639, AT II, 597f.
[4] *New Essays concerning Human Understanding*, I, ii, 20.
[5] Ibid, II, i, 2.

certain ideas imprinted on the soul at birth, or which makes of the mind what Malebranche, in attacking the doctrine of innate ideas, called 'a storehouse'. It asserts rather that in 'the acts of refection' we 'think of that which calls itself "I", and . . . observe that this or that is within us; and it is thus that in thinking of ourselves, we think of being, of substance, . . . of the immaterial. . . .'[6] Having got these ideas from the reflection on the self we can then extend them to all other beings. This theory of innateness belongs as an integral part to Leibniz's conception of consciousness or apperception. There is in Descartes also an account of innate ideas directly related to *his* conception of consciousness. We have something very close indeed to Leibniz's statement, just quoted, in Descartes' reference in *Meditation III* to certain ideas which 'seem as though I might have derived them from the idea which I possess of myself, as those which I have of substance, duration, number, and such like'. For example, if I am able to think of a stone as 'a substance, or at least as a thing capable of existing of itself', this is possible because I am conscious of myself as a substance or self-subsistent thing. Similarly, because I am conscious of existing now, and remember existing earlier, and because I am capable of enumerating my thoughts, 'I acquire ideas of duration and number which I can afterwards transfer to any object that I please'.[7] Descartes' concepts, 'substance', 'duration', 'number', which can be derived from reflection on the self are extended in *Meditation III* from the self to corporeal things. Elsewhere he refers to them along with 'existence', 'order', and 'possibly such other similar matters', as the most general concepts we have, applying to all classes of real things.[8]

Like Descartes Leibniz never gives a definitive or exhaustive list of the general concepts applicable to all beings, concepts which are discovered by reflection on the self. The most frequently named by him are 'being', 'substance', 'action', 'cause', 'unity', 'identity', 'similarity', 'duration'. On occasion he says that there are thousands of such ideas.

This version of innateness, based on consciousness or apperception, is repeated often in Leibniz's writings, but the derivation of ideas in this way is never given the detailed treatment which it

[6] *Monadology*, Section 30.
[7] AT IX, 35. HR I, 165.
[8] *Principles of Philosophy* I, 48. AT IX, 45. HR I, 238.

would seem to deserve. On the other hand, because the relation of innateness to consciousness is so closely involved in the development of the argument of the *Meditations*, there is detail in Descartes' account which is quite lacking in Leibniz's, and with Descartes there is much more to go on in considering the relation between innateness and consciousness.

It is in *Meditation III* that Descartes first mentions innate ideas, contrasting them with adventitious and fictitious ideas. He says of the innate ideas, 'for as I have the power of understanding what is called a thing, or a truth, or a thought, it appears to me that I hold this power from no other source than my own nature'.[9] The examples which are given of innate ideas, 'thing', 'truth', and 'thought', have in the context in which they appear an obvious relation to the *cogito ergo sum*. It should therefore be fruitful if we wish to determine what Descartes means by innateness, to examine the relationship of these concepts to the *cogito*. All three are involved in the experiences he has recounted of what had occurred in the first two days, and has now occurred at the beginning of the third day. On the second day Descartes began with a reflection on what had occurred on the previous day, when he 'doubted', then 'denied', and was finally 'persuaded that there was nothing. . . .' etc. He finally concluded that this proposition: I am, I exist, is necessarily true each time I pronounce it or mentally conceive it. His next question was, What am I? The answer, 'I am a thinking thing', is derived wholly from reflection on the *cogito ergo sum*. In this indubitable statement, I am a thinking thing, there are two general concepts involved: 'thing', and 'thought', two of the three which Descartes gives as examples of innate ideas. The third concept 'truth' is involved in his next reflection on the *cogito ergo sum*, which occurred at the beginning of the third day. 'I shall now look around more carefully to see whether I cannot still discover in myself some other things which I have not hitherto perceived. I am certain that I am a thing which thinks; but do I not then likewise know what is requisite to render me certain of a truth? Certainly in this first knowledge there is nothing excepting the clear and distinct perception of that which I state.'[10]

But these three are not the only concepts which Descartes

[9] AT IX, 29. HR I, 160.
[10] *Meditation* III, AT IX, 27 HR I, 157f.

D

elicited from the argument of the *cogito*. In reflecting on the experiences leading up to the assertion, 'I am, I exist', I see that I am conscious of myself as doubting and desiring to know and therefore as lacking something or as imperfect. But to be conscious of myself in this way would not be possible unless I already had the idea of the perfect being. Thus reflection on my nature as involved in the *cogito* yields a still further innate idea. Finally in *Meditation* IV reflection on the experiences leading to the 'I am, I exist', reveals the idea of freedom. It was already on the first day that Descartes had discovered that no matter how great the power of the evil genius to deceive him, he was still free to withhold his belief or to deny. This freedom of doubting and denying is experienced on the first day. The freedom of asserting is experienced on the second day, when he asserts his own existence, conscious of being uncompelled by any external cause. Freedom of the will is described as 'one of the first and most ordinary notions that are found innately in us'.[11]

How Descartes conceives the nature of the relation of these ideas to the *cogito ergo sum* becomes clearer if we look at his reply to the criticism that logically the *cogito ergo sum* cannot satisfy the requirements of a first principle, the requirement, namely, that 'There is no other principle on which it depends, nor anything which can be more readily discovered'.[12] His claim for the primitiveness of our knowledge of the *cogito ergo sum* might, he anticipates, be challenged on the ground, first, that we should have to have a prior knowledge or understanding of the concepts involved, namely, 'thought' and 'existence', and secondly, that the *cogito ergo sum* is really an enthymeme whose suppressed major premise is the general principle, 'he who thinks exists'; consequently the validity of the conclusion, 'I exist', rests on the prior knowledge of that general principle. Descartes' reply necessitates a consideration of his conception of the philosophical method which he used in the *Meditations*, a method of argument or proof which he contrasts directly with that of the syllogism. The authors of *Objections* II suggested to him that it would make things easier for his readers were he to put his argument in the form of definitions, axioms, and postulates, as premises and then go on to theorems as conclusions from these premises. For Descartes to do this would

[11] *Principles*, I, 39. AT IX, 41. HR I, 234.
[12] To Clerselier, June or July, 1646. AT IV, 444.

be, in effect, to meet the demand of the critics of the primacy of
the *cogito ergo sum* that we first need to have the definition of
'thought' and 'existence' and the axiom 'he who thinks exists',
before we can proceed to the syllogism of which 'I exist' is the
conclusion.

In response to the advice given him by the authors of *Objections
II* Descartes distinguished for them between the analytic and
synthetic method of proof, remarking that in his *Meditations* he
had used only analysis. Analysis as a method shows how a truth
is discovered, while synthesis, though it proceeds from definitions,
axioms, and postulates, to theorems and conclusions, conceals
how the truth was discovered and is useful only as a pedagogic
device for teaching to others what has already been discovered.
Descartes then obliged his critics by showing how his metaphysics
would appear when put in the synthetic form. First, he gives
definitions (including the definition of 'thought'), then postulates,
and then axioms; these are followed by propositions, each proved
in strict syllogistic form, the major and minor premises in each
syllogism being taken from the set of definitions, postulates and
axioms. Notable in this presentation is the total absence of the
cogito ergo sum in the argument.

Descartes uses the contrast between the analytical method and
the synthetical or syllogistic method to meet Gassendi's objection
that the *cogito ergo sum* implies the assumption of the major
premiss, 'he who thinks exists'. Gassendi's great error is

the assumption that the knowledge of particular truths is
always deduced from universal propositions in consonance
with the order of the sequence observed in the syllogism of
dialectic. This shows that he is but little acquainted with the
method by which truth should be investigated. For it is certain
that in order to discover the truth we should always start with
particular notions, in order to arrive at general conceptions
subsequently, though we may also in the reverse way, after
having discovered the universal deduce other particulars from
them. Thus in teaching a child the elements of geometry we
shall certainly not make him understand the general truth that
'when equals are taken from equals the remainders are equal' or
that 'the whole is greater than its parts' unless by showing him
examples in particular cases.[13]

[13] To Clerselier, 12 January, 1646. AT IX 205f, HR II, 127.

The same point is made to the author of *Objections* II:

> When we first become aware that we are thinking beings, this is a primitive act of knowledge derived from no syllogistic reasoning. He who says, '*I think, hence I am, or exist*' does not deduce existence from thought by a syllogism, but, by a simpler act of mental vision, recognizes it as if it were a thing that is known *per se*. This is evident from the fact that if it were syllogistically deduced, the major premiss, that *everything that thinks is, or exists*, would have to be known previously; but yet that has rather been learned from the experience of the individual— that unless he exists he cannot think. For our mind is so constituted by nature that general propositions are formed out of the knowledge of particulars.[14]

Descartes's account of how we come to have the knowledge of universal principles is the same as Aristotle's account of induction in the *Posterior Analytics*, the kind of induction which has aptly been called 'intuitive induction' by W. E. Johnson. For Aristotle our knowledge of the primary premises of scientific or demonstrative knowledge is derived from 'exhibiting the universal as implicit in the clearly known particular'.[15] While Descartes regards this kind of induction as including the derivation of the universals of geometry from the experience of the particular, it is, nevertheless, its role in connection with the derivation of universal concepts and principles from the *cogito* which is of paramount concern to him. The experiential character of the knowledge of the *cogito ergo sum* is vividly described to the Marquis of Newcastle. 'Will you not admit that you are less assured of the presence of the object you see than of the truth of this proposition: *I think, therefore I am*? Now this knowledge is not the product of your reasoning, nor something taught you by your masters; your mind sees it, feels it, and handles it. . . .'[16] Must we first define 'doubt', 'thought', and 'existence', before we can say 'I doubt, therefore I exist', or 'I think, therefore I exist?' 'One learns those things in no other way than by one's self and that nothing else persuades us of them except our own experience and this consciousness or internal testimony (*eaque conscientia vel interno testimonio*) that each finds within himself when he examines things.'[17]

[14]AT IX, 110f. HR II, 38.   [15]*An. Post.* 71a, 7.
[16] March or April, 1648. AT V, 138.
[17] *The Search after Truth*, AT X, 524. HR I, 324f.

Taking experience now in this special sense in which it is to be identified with consciousness, or internal testimony, we find that Descartes distinguishes within experience between the 'explicit' and the 'implicit', or between what I directly attend to and what I do not directly attend to or reflect upon. In the *Conversation with Burman*, Burman refers to Descartes' statement in *Replies* II that the *I think therefore I am* is a primitive act of thought derived from no syllogistic reasoning. Burman asks whether this is consistent with what Descartes has said in Principles, I, 10. Plainly it does seem contrary, for there Descartes said, 'When I stated that this proposition *I think, therefore I am* is the first and most certain which presents itself to those who philosophize in orderly fashion, I did not for all that deny that we must first of all know *what is knowledge, what is existence, and what is certainty*, and *that in order to think, we must be*, and such like; but because these are notions of the simplest kind, which of themselves give us no knowledge of anything that exists, I did not think them worthy of being put on record'.[18]

In reply to Burman's question Descartes says that we do need the major, *everything that thinks is*. It *is* prior to the conclusion, *I think, therefore I am*, and the conclusion depends on it. For that reason he had said in the *Principles* that it precedes 'because implicitly it is always presupposed and prior. But I do not always have an express and explicit knowledge of this priority, while I do have a prior knowledge of my conclusion because I pay attention only to that which I experience in myself, namely, *I think, therefore I am*, while I do not direct the same attention to this general notion, *everything which thinks exists*: in short, as I have pointed out, we do not separate the proposition from particular things; it is in this sense that the words quoted [from the *Principles*] should be understood.'[19]

Just as there are principles contained in our experience, principles upon which we may direct no attention nor abstract in their generality from particular things, so also there are ideas which are implicit in our experience or consciousness of ourselves, but to which we do not necessarily direct our attention nor render explicit, and on which some men will never reflect. Thus, concerning the idea of the perfect being, which is *logically* presupposed

[18] AT IX, 29. HR I, 222.
[19] *Conversation with Burman*, AT V, 147.

in my knowledge of my own imperfection, Descartes says to
Burman that although he has not recognized the perfection of
God 'explicitly', nevertheless he has 'implicitly'. 'For, explicitly,
we can know our own imperfection before the perfection of God,
because we are able to pay attention to ourselves before attending
to God, and come to see our own finitude before coming to see his
infinitude; but implicitly, the knowledge of God and of his
perfections must always precede the knowledge of ourselves and
our imperfections. For, in truth, the infinite perfection of God is
prior to our imperfection, because our imperfection is the lack or
negation of God's perfection; now, all lack, like all negation, presupposes the thing of which it is a lack or a negation.'[20]

When Descartes maintains the primitive character of the
cogito ergo sum, asserting that the general proposition *whatever
thinks exists* is derived from it, rather than *vice versa*, and adds, 'for
our mind is so constituted by nature that general propositions are
formed out of the knowledge of particulars', he is not asserting the
the logical priority of the knowledge of the particular; rather he is
concerned with the transition from the implicit to the explicit
within 'experience' or 'consciousness'. Descartes' entire activity
in the first four *Meditations* of extracting the concepts of 'thing',
'thought', 'truth', 'substance', 'God', 'freedom', is that of directing
attention to, or reflecting upon, what I am pre-reflectively conscious of in the *cogito*. It is this which constitutes the passage from
the experience of the individual to general notions and principles.
These notions are innate in the sense that they are implicit in
experience or consciousness. They are not prior to experience or
consciousness, they are prior only to reflection on experience.
Thus Descartes says

> It is indeed true that no one can be sure that he knows or that
> he exists, unless he knows what thought is and what existence is.
> Not that this requires a cognition formed by reflection or one
> acquired by demonstration; much less does it require a cognition
> of this reflective knowledge by which we know that we know,
> and again know that we know that we know and so *ad infinitum*.
> Such knowledge could never be attained of anything. It is
> altogether enough for one to know it by means of that internal
> cognition which always precedes reflective knowledge, and

[20] Ibid. AT V, 153.

which, when the object is thought and existence, is innate in all men. . . . When, therefore, anyone perceived that he thinks and that it then follows that he exists, although he chanced never previously to have asked what thought is, nor what existence, he cannot nevertheless fail to have a knowledge of each sufficient to give him an assurance on this score.[21]

Certain universal concepts such as 'thought', 'existence', 'thing', 'substance', 'duration', 'number', and the universal principle 'He who thinks exists', are all capable of being derived by intuitive induction from my experience or consciousness of *any* individual act of thinking. Every man has an implicit knowledge of these concepts from the mere fact that he thinks and is conscious of thinking. In that sense they are innate in all men. When Aristotle raised the question as to the source of our knowledge of the premises of science or demonstrative knowledge, he maintaind that these must either be innate or acquired from sense perception. He eliminated the first of these possibilities in favour of the second. When Descartes maintained that our knowledge of the principles of philosophy is innate, he plainly did not mean what Aristotle meant by innate. He meant that besides sense experience of particulars from which we derive by intuitive induction the universals of geometry, there is also the internal experience or consciousness of any individual act of thinking from which by a similar intuitive induction we can derive certain primitive notions which belong among the principles of philosophy. They are innate in that we find them in ourselves when we reflect on what is implicit in our consciousness or experience of ourselves as thinking.

There is absolutely nothing in this version of innateness to suggest that these ideas are in any way in the mind prior to its first act of thinking, or to the experience or consciousness of that act of thinking, any more than Aristotle's universals were for him in the mind prior to knowledge of the particular. They are innate only in the sense that they are found in the mind when the mind reflects on what it is already conscious of when it thinks and which is implicit in the experience of thinking. What, however, about the idea of God? Is this not an idea imprinted on the mind in its original condition? Descartes says 'One certainly ought not to find it strange that God, in creating me, placed this idea within me

[21] *Reply* VI, AT IX, 225. HR II, 241.

to be like the mark of the workman imprinted on his work'.[22]
Everything hinges on the meaning to be attached to the word
'imprinted'. Here we must note that Descartes says that the idea
of God 'is innate in me just as the idea of myself is innate in me'.[23]
He says moreover that 'it is not essential that the mark [of the
workman imprinted on his work] should be something different
from the work itself'. Thus, he explains to Gassendi, a picture
whose inimitable technique showed that it was painted by Apelles
could be said to carry the mark which Apelles imprinted on all his
pictures.[24] This makes it clear that it is *on my nature* not *in my mind*
—that God has imprinted his mark. That is why reflection on the
self of which I am conscious yields not only the idea of what I am
but the idea of God too. The two ideas are innate in the same sense.
They would not be innate in the same sense, however, if the idea
of God was an idea imprinted in the mind at birth. It is the latter
kind of innateness which Locke's polemic against innate ideas was
directed against.

The Innate Ideas of Mathematics

So far as the two sciences of arithmetic and geometry are
concerned, for both Descartes and Leibniz the concept of number,
but not that of extension, can have its origin in self-consciousness.
'When I remember,' says Descartes, 'that I have various thoughts
of which I can recognize the number I acquire the idea . . . of
number which I can afterwards transfer to any object that I
please.'[25] And Leibniz says, 'Number is perceived by all the
external senses, but because it is also perceived by the internal
sense, and even more so, *arithmetic* is more rightly subordinated to
metaphysics.'[26] The basic concept of geometry, extension, does
not have this origin in internal sense. Nevertheless both Descartes
and Leibniz maintain the innate character of the ideas of geometry.
Hence we must enquire whether the ideas of geometry are not
innate in some sense which is different from that of the general
concepts of metaphysics, including among these the concept of
number which is the foundation of arithmetic. The difficulty of

---

[22] *Meditation* III AT IX, 41. HR I, 170.
[23] Ibid.
[24] Ibid.
[25] *Meditation* III IX, 35. HR I, 165.
[26] *Method for Learning and Teaching Jurisprudence*, Part I, Section 36, revision
note. *Leibniz, Philosophical Papers and Letters*, ed. L. E. Loemker, Chicago
(1956), 557.

answering this question is accentuated by the fact that both philosophers regard the concept of extension as derived from external sense. Thus Leibniz in contrasting geometry with arithmetic observes that, although the concept of number is derived pre-eminently from internal sense, 'extension, which is perceived by sight and touch alone, involves number but adds *situation* to it, or the order of coexistence, and hence adds quality to quantity. Thus figures arise as modifications of extension; hence *geometry*.'[27]

In commenting on *Meditation III* Gassendi does not miss the opportunity of taunting Descartes with the problem of how he is going to get the idea of corporeal things—things possessing extension, figure, situation and motion—out of the idea of himself. 'I have,' says Gassendi, 'doubt only about the *ideas of corporeal things*, and this is due to the fact that there is no small difficulty in seeing how you are able *to deduce them from yourself*, and *out of the idea of yourself alone*, as long as you pose as incorporeal and consider yourself as such. For, if you have known only incorporeal substance, how can you grasp the notion of corporeal substance as well. . . ? Certainly if the mind can, out of that incorporeal substance, form the idea of corporeal substance, there is no reason why we should doubt that a blind man, even one who has been completely enshrouded in darkness from his birth, can form in his own mind the idea of light and of the colours.'[28] In reply Descartes denies having asserted '*that I deduce the ideas of material things from the mind*, as you rather insincerely here pretend I do. For afterwards I showed in express terms that they often come from bodies, and that it is owing to this that the existence of corporeal things was demonstrated.'[29] This is a denial that the idea of extension is innate, though the use of the expression, 'often come from bodies', seems to leave open the possibility of an alternative origin for the idea.

There are occasions, indeed, when Descartes maintains very explicitly that the idea of extension is innate. For example, in writing to the Princess Elizabeth, 21 May, 1643, he distinguishes three primitive notions. For bodies we have the primitive notion of extension, for the soul that of thought, and for mind and body

[27] Ibid.
[28] *Objections* V, AT VIII, 293. HR II, 163.
[29] *Reply*, V, AT VIII, 367. HR II, 217f.

as found together in the unity of a person, we have the primitive notion of their union. 'We should not look for these simple notions elsewhere than in our own soul which through its own nature possesses all of them.'[30] He is equally explicit in *Principles* II, 3. 'The perceptions of the senses tell us what is beneficial or harmful to us as being possessed of both a mind and a body, but with regard to things as they are in themselves we should rely on our understanding alone, by reflecting carefully on the ideas implanted therein by nature.'[31]

Where we should expect to find the clearest statement on the subject is in *Meditation V*, where Descartes set out to determine whether anything certain can be known regarding material things. Moreover this meditation contains one of Descartes' most important references to innate ideas. While the ideas of geometrical figures are said not to be derived from the senses nor invented by me, and hence by implication are innate, nothing is said about the source of the idea of extension itself. Descartes' first step in determining the essence of material things is 'to consider the ideas of them in so far as they are in my thoughts, and to see which of them are distinct and which confused'. 'In the first place, I am able distinctly to imagine that quantity which philosophers commonly call continuous, or the extension in length, breadth, or depth, what is in this quantity, or rather in the object to which it is attributed.'[32] Descartes says, 'imagine', not 'conceive'. It might be said that he was using the word 'imagine' in a loose way in which ordinarily it covers 'think of' or 'conceive', except for the fact that in the next *Meditation* he carefully explains how different the two are. To *imagine* a triangle is not to *conceive* it as a figure enclosed by three straight lines, but to have the three straight lines present before the mind's eye. Imagining seems to involve the body, and it may be because of our relation to the body that we are able to imagine corporeal things; 'so that this mode of thinking differs from pure intellection only inasmuch as mind in conceiving in some manner turns on itself and considers some of the ideas which it possesses in itself; while in imagining it turns toward the body, and there beholds something conformable to the idea which it has either conceived of itself or perceived

[30] AT III, 665.
[31] AT IX, 64f. HR I, 255.
[32] AT IX, 50. HR I, 179.

by the senses'.[33] The extension which he examines in *Meditation V* is extension as visualized or imaged. This would be in accordance with the rule he has laid down in the *Regulae*; 'if the understanding proposes to examine something that can be referred to the body, we must form the idea of that thing as distinctly as possible in the imagination'.[34] He does not say whether this imagined extension is, in the words of the next *Meditation*, something 'conformable to the idea which the mind has conceived of itself, or perceived by the senses'. Descarte's datum is extension as imaged or visualized. Given this imaged extension, he finds that he can number in it different parts and attribute to its parts an infinitude of particulars respecting numbers, figures, movements, and other such things 'whose truth is so manifest and so well accords with my nature, that when I begin to discover them, it seems to me that I learn nothing new, or recollect what I formerly knew—that is to say, that I for the first time perceive things which were already present to my mind, although I had not as yet applied my mind to them'.[35]

The first thing clearly and distinctly perceived in extension is its divisibility. From this all the rest follows. For if it is divisible, then extension contains within it the unlimited possibilities of parts possessing different sizes, figures, situations and local motions, and from these I can go on to make an infinitude of discoveries respecting numbers, figures, and motions. Thus there arises the whole science of geometry in which as I proceed deductively 'it seems to me that I learn nothing new but recollect what I formerly knew'.

According to this account the whole of geometry may be described as innate in that it draws out by deduction what is implicit in an idea already existing in the mind, that of extension. But the question still remains untouched, is the idea of extension itself, on which all the rest depends, innate or is it acquired? The answer in the next *Meditation* is quite clear: it is acquired through the senses. God has given me a very strong inclination to believe that my ideas of corporeal things are caused in me by corporeal things themselves, hence 'I do not see how he could be defended from the accusation of deceit if those ideas were produced by

[33] *Meditation* VI. AT IX, 58. HR I, 186.
[34] *Rule* XII. AT X, 416f. HR I, 40.
[35] *Meditation,* V. AT IX, 50. HR I, 179.

causes other than corporeal objects'.[36] Our idea of bodies as extended comes from bodies acting on us through the senses. Much that comes to us through the senses, however, is obscure. That is why at the beginning of *Meditation V* Descartes' first task was to separate out what is distinct in our ideas of body from what is obscure. And in *Meditation VI*, after unequivocally asserting that the idea of extension is produced in us by bodies, and is therefore not innate, he goes on to warn that 'they are not always perhaps just as we perceive them by the senses, for sense perception is in many cases obscure and confused; but at least it can be said that everything in them which I clearly and distinctly conceive, that is to say everything which is comprised within the subject of pure mathematics, is truly to be found in them.'[37]

The distinction made between clear and distinct ideas on the one hand, and obscure and confused on the other, is not the same as that between innate ideas and adventitious ideas, or ideas derived from the senses. The latter distinction is one between two kinds of ideas according to their origin. The former distinction is based on differences of degree, and can be found within all perception, whether the ideas involved are adventitious or innate. The work of attending and distinguishing whereby what we perceive is made clear and distinct is the work of the *understanding* as opposed to the senses, but this work of the understanding can equally well be directed at either the innate or the adventitious.

When Descartes describes in *Meditation V* a kind of knowledge which is drawn out of his mind by invoking the simile of reminiscence he is not, then, referring to ideas which are got by reflecting on his own nature as he does in the first four *Meditations*. Nor is the simile of reminiscence appropriate to that earlier account of innateness. Descartes means something quite different from what is discovered by reflection on the self when he says in *Meditation V* concerning the concepts of geometry 'I for the first time perceive things which were already present to my mind, although I had not yet applied my mind to them'. This statement is best understood by the contrast of these ideas with adventitious and factitious ideas. In the first place they stand contrasted with adventitious ideas in that they are not derived from the senses. For while the idea of extension itself be adventitious, my ideas of the infinity of

[36]AT IX, 63. HR I, 191.
[37] Ibid.

possible figures in extension are not. On the contrary they are the *logical* consequence of the divisibility which I clearly and distinctly perceive in extension. In the second place these ideas stand contrasted with factitious ideas, in that the various properties of these figures, as for example, in the case of the triangle, that its three angles are equal to two right angles, are not invented by me, but are *logically* determined by the nature of the figures, or in Descartes' words: 'I can nevertheless demonstrate various properties pertaining to their nature as well as to that of the triangle'. Leibniz too sometimes quite directly takes knowledge through demonstrative proof as what is meant by the term innate. This is the import of his use of the analogy of reminiscence. 'It must be said that all arithmetic and all geometry are innate, and are in us virtually, so that we can find them there if we consider attentively and set in order what we already have in the mind without making use of any truth learned through experience or through the tradition of another, as Plato has shown in a dialogue in which he introduces Socrates leading a child to abstruse truths by questions alone without giving him any information. We can, then, make for ourselves these sciences in our study, and even with closed eyes, without learning through sight or even through touch the truths which we need . . . .'[38]

If Descartes regards the ideas and truths of geometry as innate in the mind they are so in the sense that they are *logically* entailed by an idea which is in the mind, namely extension, without reference, however, to whether the idea of extension itself originates in sense experience or not. That it does originate in sense experience is irrelevant to this conception of innateness, as is the case also for Leibniz.

It will be useful here to note that Spinoza was just as concerned as either Descartes or Leibniz with the contrast between logically derived knowledge, 'which depends on the actual power and nature of the understanding', and the empirically given, that is knowledge which is 'determined by an external object'.[39] The soul acting according to to 'its own fixed laws', the laws of logic, is described accordingly by Spinoza as 'an immaterial automaton', an expression which Leibniz approved so much that he adopted it for his own use. No one, on the basis of this description of the

[38] *New Essays* I, i, 5.
[39] *Treatise on the Improvement of the Understanding*, Section 71.

mind's power 'to arrive at knowledge independently of the senses', has, so far as I know, attributed a doctrine of innateness to Spinoza, even if what he taught here is identical with what Descartes and Leibniz designated as 'innate'. Indeed one may wonder why the two latter called logically derived knowledge innate except for its striking resemblance to recollection, which provided the earliest form of a theory of innate knowledge.

Professor Vlastos in *Anamnesis in the Meno* maintains that Leibniz correctly interpreted the Platonic doctrine of anamnesis. 'Reduced to its simplest terms what Plato means by "recollection" in the *Meno* is *any enlargement of our knowlege which results from the perception of logical relationships*. When these are inter-propositional to "recollect" a previously unknown proposition is to come to know it by seeing that it is entailed by others already known. Or if the relations are intra-propositional, as in the case of the true answer to the "What is X?" question, then to "recollect" is to gain insight into the logical structure of a concept, so that when faced with its correct definition one will see the concepts mentioned are analytically connected'.[40] Plato's 'assertion that to acquire knowledge is only to recover what is already "in" us could not but have the force of an implicit denial that *knowledge can be acquired by sense experience* . . . Plato's formula is equivalent to the denial that sense-experience can, or need, provide the slightest evidence for propositions known in the special way in which knowledge is here construed: demonstrative knowledge.'[41]

I leave aside the question whether Professor Vlastos is right in saying that this is what Plato meant by recollection. But he is right in saying that this is how Leibniz interpreted the doctrine of recollection, and he could perfectly well have added that this is what Descartes meant when he used the expression 'seem to recollect'. Both Descartes and Leibniz reject, of course, the notion that the soul acquired its mathematical knowledge in a precedent existence. In the fifth *Meditation*'s account of innate knowledge as quasi recollection, there are no geometrical ideas in the mind prior to the mind's first sensible experience of extension.

Innate Ideas as Tendencies or Dispositions

Confronted with the obvious fact that we learn as we grow and that the newly born infant is in a state of virtually complete

[40] *Dialogue* vol. IV, No. 2, 156.
[41] Ibid. 16of.

ignorance, there was a natural propensity for defenders of innate
ideas to explain them as innate faculties, dispositions, or tendencies,
which come into play as occasion arises and as life goes on. For
this Locke had small respect. 'To say a notion is imprinted on the
mind, and yet at the same time to say that the mind is ignorant of
it, and never yet took notice of it, is to make this impression
nothing . . . . If the capacity of knowing be the natural impression
contended for, all the truths a man ever comes to know will, by
this account, be everyone of them innate; and this great point will
amount to no more, but only to a very improper way of speaking;
which whilst it pretends to assert the contrary, says nothing different from those who deny innate principles. For nobody, I think,
ever denied that the mind was capable of knowing several truths.
The capacity they say is innate, the knowledge acquired. But then
to what end such contest for certain innate maxims'.[42]

The *tabula rasa* conception of the mind which Locke espoused
allows, of course, that all knowledge exists potentially in the mind,
for the blank sheet of paper or wax tablet has the capacity or
faculty for receiving any figures whatever which will be imprinted
or impressed on it in the fullness of time. But such potentiality
Locke justly considered hardly worth mentioning. If we revert
now to what Descartes has to say about ideas in relation to faculties
or innate capacities we find that he differs hardly at all from Locke.
In a letter in which Descartes compares his own views with those
in *De Veritate* of Lord Herbert he refers, among other things, to
their differing conceptions of faculties. 'He [Lord Herbert]
would have it that there are as many faculties in us as there are
diversities of things to be known, which I can only understand to
be like saying that, because wax can receive an infinitude of shapes,
it has within it an infinitude of faculties for receiving them. In a
sense this is true, but I do not see that anything useful can be had
from such a way of speaking. That is why I prefer to conceive
that wax, by virtue of its flexibility alone, receives all kinds of
shapes, and that the mind acquires all its knowledge by its reflection, either upon itself for intellectual objects, or upon the various
dispositions of the brain, to which it is joined, for corporeal
objects, whether these dispositions depend on the senses or on
other causes.'[43]

[42] *Essay*, I, ii, 5.
[43] To Mersenne, 16 October, 1639. AT II, 598.

This is not the only occasion on which Descartes makes use of the conception of the mind as a *tabula rasa*. 'There is for me no other difference between the soul and its ideas than there is between a piece of wax and the various figures which it can receive. And just as it is not properly an action, but a passion in the wax, to receive various figures, it seems to me that it is similarly a passion in the soul to receive this or that idea, and that it is only its volitions which are actions.'[44] Descartes used the *tabula rasa* analogy in his early work, the *Regulae,* where it is worked out in detail. In the first of the letters quoted he has been careful to maintain his distinctions of ideas as innate, adventitious and fictitious. The innate are those which the mind 'acquires' (Descartes' word) from reflection on itself. We have already considered what this means. The adventitious and fictitious ideas are those which it 'acquires' from attending to images in the brain. In the case of adventitious ideas the images have been impressed on the brain by external objects acting through the organs of sense. In the case of fictitious or imaginary ideas the images have been imprinted on the brain by the mind itself, that is, the mind gives the images to itself. But in all cases the mind acquires its ideas by attending to something present to it.

There is, however, an account of innate ideas in Descartes' *Notes Directed against a Certain Programme* which appears to be markedly at variance with the views which have just been considered, and which appears to identify the innateness of ideas with the innateness of specific and active faculties, tendencies, or dispositions. In the *Notes,* Descartes protests that he has never maintained that innate ideas are in any way different from the faculty of thinking itself. Ideas are innate in the same sense as when we say that 'in some families generosity is innate, in others certain diseases like gout or gravel, not that on this account the babes of these families suffer from these diseases in their mother's womb, but because they are born with a certain disposition or propensity for contracting them.' In likening these dispositions or tendencies of the mind to those of the body to contract certain diseases, Descartes seems to suggest that these specific potentialities are passive, but then as he goes on he seems to be arguing, on the grounds of the unlikeness between our ideas of things and what is presented to us through the senses, that the dispositions

[44] To Mesland, 2 May, 1644 (?) AT IV, 113f.

are active, and that moreover, there are no ideas which are not innate as active dispositions. 'In our ideas there is nothing which was not innate in the mind, or faculty of thinking, except only those circumstances which point to experience—the fact, for instance, that we judge that this or that idea, which we now have present to our thought, is to be referred to a certain extraneous thing, not that these extraneous things transmitted the ideas themselves to our minds through the organs of sense, but because they transmitted something which gave the mind occasion to form these ideas, by means of an innate faculty, at this time rather than at another. For nothing reaches our mind from external objects through the organs of sense but certain corporeal movements— but even these movements, and the figures which arise from them, are not conceived by us in the shape they assume in the organs of sense, as I have explained in my *Dioptrics*. Hence it follows that the ideas of the movements and figures are themselves innate in us. So much the more must the ideas of pain, colour, sound and the like be innate, that our mind may on occasion of certain corporeal movements, envisage these ideas, for they have no likenesses to the corporeal movements.'[45]

The difference between the forming of ideas and the occasions for forming them is for Descartes the same as that between the proximate or primary cause of a thing and its remote or accidental cause, the latter providing the former with the occasion for producing its effects at one time rather than at another. Workmen are the proximate or primary causes of what they produce. Those who commission their work are the accidental or remote causes, without which the work would never have been produced.

We seem, then, to be confronted with two quite different causal accounts of ideas. On the one hand there is the causal account of ideas according to the *tabula rasa* conception of the mind; on the other we *seem* to have one in which the mind is conceived as possessing certain specific dispositions to knowledge. By the latter, instead of the mind receiving its ideas, whether innate or adventitious, the mind *acts* as circumstances provide the occasion. Ideas would be powers or dispositions or pre-determinations in the mind, native to it, to act in certain ways. Thus all ideas would be innate. There would be no adventitious ideas, for no ideas would be acquired.

[45]AT VIII, 357f. HR I, 442f.

E

This second version of innateness which Descartes *seems* to maintain in the *Notes* was one which Leibniz was to elaborate in the *New Essays*, and what Descartes says in the *Notes* is strikingly similar to what Leibniz was later to say. Moreover, it was certainly the version of innateness which was to be presented by so faithful a follower of Descartes as La Forge who no doubt derived it from the *Notes*. We must not, however, fail to observe that in putting it forward, La Forge had to introduce a very significant modification into Descartes' use of the wax analogy. 'Ideas,' La Forge says, 'are contained in the mind only in potency, and not in act, almost in the way in which figures are contained in the wax, with this difference, however, that in the wax this potency is merely passive, while in the soul it is also active.'[46]

Are we justified in accepting what might be called the La Forge interpretation of the account of innateness given in the *Notes*? There seems to be at least two strong reasons for not accepting it. In the first place it is, as noted already, so completely at odds with Descartes' reiterated use elsewhere of the wax analogy for conceiving the nature of the mind, and in the second place, it is not borne out by the *Dioptrics*. This is where we should go if we wish to understand what is said in the *Notes*, for it will be noticed that Descartes says in the *Notes* that he had already explained himself at great length in the *Dioptrics*—a work in which he was concerned with perceptual judgments.

In this latter work Descartes tells us that we must not think of an image as a copy or resemblance or picture in the head, but as something analogous to signs or words. Vision to be properly understood must be thought of in the way a blind man with a stick is able, from the resistance offered to it, to observe all sorts of differences between trees, stones, water, and so on, differences which are just as great for him as those between different colours, for the man who can see. The blind man obviously operates with signs, not resemblances.

For Descartes all perceivable qualities in the objects of sight can be reduced to six principal ones: light, colour, position, distance, size and shape. Through colour, he says, we are able to distinguish the parts of a body. He then goes on to show first that our knowledge of the position of an object does not depend on any image, and secondly that the perception of distance does

---

[46] *Traité de l'esprit de l'homme*, Geneva (1725), 25.

not depend on any image, and thirdly, that our perceptions of size and shape are *a fortiori* not determined by any images, since they are determined by the way we see the distance and position of the parts of the object. The perception of these latter four qualities of the object are judgments which the mind makes on the basis of sensory data—sensory data which function for it as signs, not copes or resemblances. The signs give the mind the occasion for judging or, in the language of the *Notes*, the occasion to form these ideas by means of an innate faculty. It is the faculty of judging which is innate to the mind, and if we speak of the conceptions which we form through judgment as innate, it is only because they are formed by that innate faculty, not produced by what comes through the senses. It is impossible to read into the *Dioptrics* any conception of ideas as innate active dispositions. They are not potencies prior to acts of judgment. They are products of judgment. We cannot, therefore, on the basis of the *Notes against a Programme* turn Descartes into a kind of Leibnizian. Their conceptions of the mind are completely different.

Reference was made at the beginning to *three* senses of innateness. Plainly, eliciting certain ideas by reflecting on myself as thinking is very different from determining that the interior angles of a triangle are equal to two right angles, and these in turn are both different from determining the real position, distance, shape and size of a perceptual object. Are we to say that the only thing that unites the three is that in none of them are my ideas produced by the senses? What unites them is much stronger than that. In the first of the three we have a case of simple intuition. In reflecting on itself as thinking the pure and attentive mind sees what is implicit in the individual act of thinking. The mind does no more than *attend*—a word which is much emphasized in the *Conversation with Burman*. It is merely attention which renders the implicit explicit. In the second case the mind arrives at certain ideas by exercising a logical function of deducing, e.g. deducing the properties of a triangle from its nature. In the third the mind performs the logical deductions of a detective, who uses certain clues provided by the senses to determine the actual position, shape and size of an object. In Rule III, Descartes maintains that there are only two ways by which we can arrive at the knowledge of things, intuition and deduction. He then, however, goes on to say that the steps in a deductive chain are nothing but a series of intuitions. Thus all that the understanding is capable of reduces to the one thing, vision. If this is so then there is no room here for any conception of ideas as part of the original equipment or possessions of the mind, or as predeterminations of what it will think. On the contrary, what it will think will be entirely determined by what it will see. It will see clearly and distinctly or obscurely and confusedly to the degree to which it attends.

III

DESCARTES' DEFINITION OF THOUGHT

Robert McRae

Descartes defines thought in this way:

> Thought is a word that covers everything that exists in us in such a way that we are immediately conscious of it. Thus all the operations of the will, intellect, imagination, and of the senses are thoughts.[1]

For such distinguished Cartesian scholars as Gilson, Laporte and Alquié, this definition asserts that thought is simply a synonym for consciousness.[2]

There is another view of what Descartes meant by thought taken by some scholars which is closely related to the one just cited, but which must be distinguished from it. This time it is not the word 'conscious' in the definition which is remarked, but the list of things included under thought which Descartes gives in *Meditation* II. 'What is a thing which thinks?' he asks. 'It is a thing which doubts, understands, affirms, denies, wills, refuses, which also imagines and feels'. Thus Koyré in his introduction to Anscombe's and Geach's translation of Descartes' writings maintains that in order to do justice to the far wider use of the

[1] *Reply* II, def. I AT VII, 160, HR II, 52. The Latin, 'ut ejus immediate conscii simus', is given in the French translation as 'que nous en sommes immédiatement connaissants'. AT IX, 124. See also *Principles* I, ix, AT VIII, 7. HR I, 222. In the French translations of Descartes' Latin which were approved by himself, the word *conscience* is avoided, with this exception in *Reply* III: 'Entendre, vouloir, imaginer, sentir, etc., conviennent entre eux en ce qu'ils ne peuvent être sans pensée, ou perception, ou conscience et connaissance.' AT IX. 137. G. Lewis remarks that this is perhaps the first use in French of the word *conscience* in a non-moral sense. *Le problème de l'inconscient et le cartésianisme*, Paris (1950), 39.

[2] E. Gilson, *Discours de la Méthode, commentaire*, Paris (1947) 293; J. Laporte, *Le Rationalisme de Descartes*, Paris (1950), 78; *Descartes, Oeuvres philosophiques* ed. F. Alquié, Paris (1963, 1967), Vol. II, 586 n. The passage from *Reply* III quoted in Note 1, above, makes *conscience* a synonym of *pensée*, as does also Descartes' phrase, 'ma propre pensée ou conscience', in a letter to Gibieuf, 19 January, 1642. AT III, 474. It may, however, be questioned whether the *definitions* of thought given in *Reply* II and *Principles* I, ix, make the two terms synonymous.

word *thought* prevalent in the seventeenth century 'we have in most cases to render "thought" by "consciousness".'[3] This decision is clearly reflected in the translation by Anscombe and Geach.

It is possible that 'consciousness' is the best contemporary idiomatic expression to convey what was called 'thought' by Descartes. At least 'consciousness' is widely used in this way by philosophers of very different philosophical persuasions. Consider this passage by a writer of plain English. G. E. Moore says, 'We believe that we men, besides having bodies, also have *minds*; and one of the chief things which we mean, by saying we have *minds*, is, I think, this: namely, that we perform certain mental acts or acts of consciousness. That is to say, we see and hear and feel and remember and imagine and think and believe and desire and like and dislike and will and love and are angry and afraid, etc. These things that we do are all of them mental acts—acts of mind or *consciousness*; whenever we do any of them, we are conscious of something; each of them partly consists in our being conscious of something in some way or other: and it seems to me that the things of which we are most certain, when we say that we are certain that we have minds, is that we do these things—that we perform these acts of consciousness.'[4]

Those who share this use of the term *consciousness* with G. E. Moore and with many others, going back in English to at least James Mill, would, of course, be justified in rendering Descartes' seventeenth century *penser* or *cogitare* into English as *to be conscious of*. But this would produce an awkward problem, for in translating Descartes' definition of thought from Latin into English, *cogitatio* would be rendered as *consciousness*, thus making it impossible to render *ut ejus immediate conscii simus* by *that we are immediately conscious of it*—for the expression *conscious* would already have been used up.

As for the first thesis, that in his definition of thought Descartes is asserting that *thought* is a synonym of *consciousness*, it is evident that this cannot be so, for he gives to each a different object. For Descartes, what I am conscious of, is what exists in me. What I am thinking, i.e. what I am doubting, affirming, denying, imagin-

[3] *Descartes, Philosophical Writings*, tr. and ed. Elizabeth Anscombe and P. T. Geach, Edinburgh (1954), xxxvii, n. 2; see also 'Translator's Note', xlviif.
[4] *Some Main Problems of Philosophy*, New York (1953), 16.

ing, perceiving or feeling, when I am thinking of 'the heavens, the earth, colours, figures, sound and all other external things' are plainly not what exists in me.

Taking our departure from Descartes' definition of thought we can say that the difference between thought and consciousness can be expressed in these two kinds of sentences:

(a) I think.

(b) I am conscious that I think.

For the variable 'think', in both of these sentences can be substituted the values 'doubt', 'understand', 'affirm', 'deny', 'desire', 'refuse', 'imagine', 'see', 'hear', 'feel'. No term other than a synonym can be substituted for 'am conscious'.

All 'thoughts' according to Descartes belong to one or the other of two kinds: perceptions of the understanding such as sensing, imagining, and conceiving; or actions of the will, such as desiring, holding in aversion, affirming, denying, doubting. In the *Passions of the Soul* he refers to these two kinds of thoughts as being respectively the passions and the actions of the soul. Thus we see that consciousness is for Descartes the kind of knowledge we attribute to agents. To be conscious is pre-eminently to know what we are doing or to know what is happening to us.

There are at least three things related to Descartes' definition of thought, which deserve to be considered. The first is that consciousness would appear by virtue of the word 'immediately' to demarcate for Descartes an area of absolute certitude, one which he totally exempts from hyperbolical doubt. The second is his denial that we can have any thoughts, in his very wide sense of thought, of which we are not conscious. The third is that being conscious of whatever exists in us is not the same as thinking of what exists in us.

First, the infallibility of consciousness which provides Descartes with the initial certainty on which his whole metaphysics rests: If I think X, then there are three things of which I am conscious, and accordingly three things of which I am certain: (1) that it is *I* who think X, (2) that I am *thinking* X, (3) that *X* is what I am thinking. None of these comes under the hyperbolical doubt.

Am I not that being who now doubts nearly everything, who nevertheless understands certain things, who affirms that one only is true, who denies all the others, who desires to know more, is averse from being deceived, who imagines many things, sometimes indeed despite his will, and who perceives many likewise, as by the intervention of the bodily organs? Is there nothing in all this which is as true as it is certain that I exist, even though I should always sleep and though he who has given me being employed all his ingenuity in deceiving me? Is there likewise any one of these attributes which can be distinguished from my thought, or which might be said to be separated from myself? For it is so evident of itself that it is I who doubts, who understands, and who desires, that there is no reason here to add anything to explain it. And I have certainly the power of imagining likewise; for although it may happen (as I formerly supposed) that none of the things which I imagine are true, nevertheless this power of imagining does not cease to be really in use, and it forms part of my thought. Finally, I am the same who feels, that is to say, who perceives certain things, as by the organs of sense, since in truth I see light, I hear noise, I feel heat. But it will be said that these phenomena are false and that I am dreaming. Let it be so; still it is at least quite certain that it seems to me that I see light, that I hear noise and that I feel heat. That cannot be false; properly speaking it is what is in me called feeling; and used in this precise sense that is no other thing than thinking.[5]

Thus (1) 'It is evident of itself that it is *I* who doubts, who desires, and who understands.'[6] (2) There is no uncertainty as to what I am doing. No question can arise as to whether I am really doubting rather than, say, affirming, desiring, or denying, or imagining, or perceiving. Each of these is exactly what we are conscious of it as being. The *dubito ergo sum* absolutely rests on this certainty. In the *Search after Truth*, Polyander says, 'I can state for certain that I never doubted what doubt is, although I never began to know it, or rather to think of it until the time when Epistemon desired to place it in doubt. You no sooner showed me the small amount of certainty which we have as to the existence of things which are only known to us by the evidence of the senses, than I commenced to doubt of them, and that sufficed to make me know doubt and at the same time my certainty of it, in such a way that I can affirm that as soon as I commenced to doubt I com-

---

[5] *Meditation* II, AT VII, 28f. HR I, 153.
[6] '. . . it is impossible that we could ever think of anything without having at the same time the idea of our soul as a thing capable of thinking everything which we think.' To Mersenne, July 1641, AT III, 394.

menced to know with certainty. But my doubt and certainty did not relate to the same object; my doubt regarded only things which existed outside me, my certainty concerned me and my doubt.'[7] What can be said of doubting, or affirming, or denying can be said of understanding or knowing. It is not by the application of external criteria that I know that I know, any more than I know that I doubt. (3) As for what I am thinking, Descartes says, 'Of my thoughts some are, so to speak, images of things, and to these alone is the title "idea" properly applied; examples are my thought of a man or of a chimera, of heaven, of an angel, or even of God. . . . Now as to what concerns ideas, if we consider them only in themselves, and do not relate them to anything beyond themselves,—they cannot properly speaking be false; for whether I imagine a goat or a chimera, it is not less true that I imagine one than the other.'[8] It is only in my judgments, according to Descartes, that falsity can lie. If, however, p is what I judge, that p is what I judge remains certain, no matter how false p may be.

It has been noted that under the heading 'thought', Descartes puts everything of which I am conscious as operating in me, either in the form of action or passion. This is not to say that I am conscious of everything that operates in me. He is careful to state to what extent my actions are the object of consciousness.

For if I say I see, or I walk, I therefore am, and if by seeing and walking I mean the action of my eyes or my legs, which is the work of my body, my conclusion is not absolutely certain. . . . But if I mean only to talk of my sensation, or my consciousness of seeing or walking, it becomes quite true because my assertion refers only to my mind, which alone is concerned with my feeling or thinking that I see and I walk.[9]

When defining 'thought' in *Replies II* as 'a word that covers everything that exists in us in such a way that we are immediately conscious of it', he emphasizes that he has said *immediately* in order to exclude those bodily movements which are a consequence of decision. Such acts depend on thought as to their cause but do not themselves come under the heading of thought.

[7] AT X, 524f, HR I, 325.
[8] *Meditation* III, AT VII, 37, HR I, 159.
[9] *Principles* I, ix, AT VIII, 7. HR I, 222.

In the definition of thought as embracing everything which exists in *me* in such a way that I am conscious of it, Descartes does not mean exclusively by *me*, *my mind*. It is true that by the end of *Meditation* II all he knows of himself with certainty is that he is a thing which thinks. But in *Meditation* VI he knows now with certainty that he is a human being, not just a thing which thinks, i.e., he knows 'what everyone always experiences in himself without philosophizing, namely, that he is a single person, who has both a body and thought, and that these are of such a nature that this thought can move the body and feel what is happening to it.'[10]

If, then, thought is everything which exists in me in such a way that I am conscious of it, the *me* is finally a person, not just a mind. Now he can say, 'there are certain things which we experience in ourselves, and which should be attributed neither to the mind nor body alone, but to the close and intimate union that exists between the mind and the body. . . . Such are the appetites of hunger, thirst, etc., and also the emotions of passions of the mind, which do not subsist in mind or thought alone, as the emotions of anger, joy, sadness, love, etc.; and finally all the sensations such as pain, pleasure, light and colour, sounds, odours, taste, heat, hardness, and all other tactile qualities.'[11]

Appetites, emotions, and sensations are all the objects of an infallible consciousness; we experience them in ourselves, but the self to which they are referred is not a mind nor a body, but the union which constitutes a person. Besides these there are, of course, acts of which we are conscious and which are acts of the mind alone, such as understanding, doubting, affirming, denying, but there are also some things which can be attributed to my body alone, and these do not come within the scope of the consciousness of what is occurring in me. With them certainty ends. My body taken without relation to the mind is only one body among others in the world, and my knowledge of it is subject to the same uncertainty as my knowledge of them. Viewed without relation to a mind, walking consists only in the motion of a body, and from this motion nothing about my existence follows. But what I am *conscious* of in walking is what Descartes, in his larger sense of the word, calls 'thought', a mode of thought which has to be referred to

---

[10] To Princess Elizabeth, 28 June, 1643. AT III, 694.
[11] *Principles*, I, xlviii. AT VIII, 23. HR I, 238.

the union of mind and body and not to mind alone. As such it can be subsumed under the word 'think' in 'I think, therefore, I am'. Taken as what I am immediately conscious of in myself there is no difference between 'I walk' and 'I think I walk', between 'I see light' and 'it seems to me I see light'.

An obvious objection likely to be made to this doctrine of the infallibility of consciousness is that in the case of such things as believing, or desiring, or undergoing certain emotions, people are far from being certain of *what* they believe, or even realizing that they *believe* it, and that the same is true of desires. As for the emotions, what can be more puzzling sometimes than what it is we really feel? Did Descartes think that all beliefs, desires and emotions are objects of an infallible consciousness, or did he just ignore the question? He by no means ignored it. He remarks in the *Discourse on Method* that in order to determine what people really believed, he 'should observe what they did rather than what they said, not only because in the corrupt state of our manners there are few people who desire to say all that they believe, but also because many are themselves ignorant of their beliefs. For since the act of thought by which we believe a thing is different from that by which we know that we believe it, the one often exists without the other'.[12] As for the emotions, or passions, under which he includes desires, Descartes, after saying 'we cannot be deceived regarding the passions, inasmuch as they are so close to, and so entirely within our soul, that it is impossible for it to feel them without their being actually such as it feels them to be',[13] nevertheless goes on to say, only two articles later, 'Experience shows us that those who are most agitated by their passions are not those who know them best'.[14]

Let us leave this puzzle for the present and go on to consider the second of Descartes' theses, which is closely related to that of infallibility, namely, that there are no thoughts in us of which we are not conscious. Arnauld interpreted Descartes as saying in the *Meditations* 'that nothing exists in him in so far as he is a thinking thing of which he is not conscious'. Descartes replied that this was self-evident. How much, then, was he claiming? 'Who has ever,' he said, 'had such an acquaintance with anything as to

[12] AT VI, 23 HR I, 95.
[13] *The Passions of the Soul*, I, xxvi. AT, XI, 348. HR I, 343.
[14] Ibid. I, xxviii. AT XI, 349. HR I, 344.

know that there is nothing in it of which he was not aware?'[15] At
the conclusion of *Meditation* II, in which he is concerned with
showing that the mind is more easily known than the body, he
speaks of his coming to know more and more about the properties
of the mind as he considers the ways in which he comes to determine the nature of wax.   When Descartes says, then, that there is
nothing in him in so far as he is a thinking thing of which he is not
conscious, he is not referring to the mind's properties or powers.
This point is made clearly in his reply to Arnauld's objection that
there may be in the mind much of which the mind is not conscious,
e.g., the infant in the womb possesses the faculty of thought
without being conscious of it.   Arnauld adds that there are
innumerable other instances which he will pass by in silence.
Descartes replies:

> There can exist in us no thought of which, at the very
> moment that it is present to us, we are not conscious.   Wherefore
> I have no doubt that the mind begins to think at the same time
> that it is infused into the body of an infant, and is at the same
> time conscious of its thought, though afterwards it does not
> remember that, because the specific forms of these thoughts do
> not live in the memory.   But it has to be noted that, while
> indeed we are always in actuality conscious of acts or operations
> of the mind, that is not the case with the faculties or powers of
> mind, except potentially.   So that when we dispose ourselves to
> the exercise of any faculty, if the faculty reside in us, we are
> immediately conscious of it; and hence we can deny that it
> exists in the mind, if we can form no consciousness of it.[16]

There are then no *actions* of the mind of which we are not immediately conscious.   But of the properties or powers of the
mind we can be unconscious until we exercise them.   Nevertheless there are no powers of the mind which we cannot ever come
to know or which are in principle unknowable.   In the account
of Descartes' conception of consciousness we can now add to
consciousness of the mind's acts, the consciousness of its powers
when these have once been brought into play.
     The principle contained in the statement: 'When we dispose
ourselves to the exercise of any faculty, if the faculty reside in us,

[15] *Reply* II. AT VII, 129. HR II, 31.
[16] *Reply* IV. AT VII, 246. HR II, 115.

we are immediately conscious of it, and hence we can deny that it exists in the mind if we can form no consciousness of it,' performs a crucial role at two points in the arguments of the *Meditations*. In the proof of the existence of God in *Meditation* III Descartes considers the possibility that he has always existed and hence does not need a God to account for his existence. He observes that from the fact that I was in existence a short time ago it does not follow that I must be in existence now, unless some cause at this instant, so to speak, produces me anew, that is to say, conserves me . . . . All that I thus require here is that I should interrogate myself if I wish to know whether I possess a power which is capable of bringing it to pass that I who am now shall still be in the future; for since I am nothing but a thinking thing, or since thus far it is only this portion of myself which is precisely in question at present, if such a power did reside in me, I should certainly be conscious of it. But I experience nothing of the kind, and by this I know clearly that I depend on some being different from myself.'[17]

The principle is invoked again in *Meditation* VI, in the proof of the existence of material things. Descartes is conscious of a certain passive faculty of perception. There must therefore be, either in himself or in something else an active power of producing the ideas of sensible things in him, 'But this active faculty cannot exist in me [inasmuch as I am a thing that thinks] seeing that it does not presuppose thought, and also that those ideas are produced in me without my contributing in any way to the same, and often even against my will: it is thus necessarily the case that the faculty resides in some substance different from me, . . .'[18] Descartes is here conscious of not contributing to the production of these ideas in himself. Therefore the faculty of producing them is not in him.

The clear statement which Arnauld elicited from Descartes, and Locke's statement that 'Whilst (the soul) thinks and perceives

---

[17] AT VII, 49. HR I, 168f.
[18] AT VII, 79. HR I, 191. In 'Descartes on Unknown Faculties: An Essential Inconsistency,' *Journal of the History of Philosophy*, vol. VI, July 1968, No. 3, 245-256. D. F. Norton points to an inconsistency in *Meditation* III where Descartes says of the ideas which appear to proceed from objects outside him, 'perhaps there is in me some faculty fitted to produce these ideas without the assistance of any external things, even though it is not yet known by me'. Yet later he goes on to say that the power of self-preservation is not in him, because if it were he would certainly be conscious of it.

. . . it must necessarily be conscious of its own perceptions,'[19] came under an historically important attack from Leibniz, who maintained that there are many perceptions within us of which we are unconscious. It might perhaps be said at once that Descartes renders his position unassailable in principle by definition. If we mean by thought anything of which I am conscious as operating in me, then anything of which I am not conscious is not what is meant by thought, and this, of course, includes all perceptions and appetites. However, it may serve to make Descartes' position clearer if we consider it in terms of Leibniz's criticism. The first thing to be noted in this one-sided controversy is that Leibniz does not maintain that there are any thoughts of which we are unconscious, but only that there are perceptions and appetites of which we are unconscious. This is evident from Leibniz's own definition of thought. In speaking of perception as the representation of the many in the one, he says. 'The possibility of such a representation of several things cannot be doubted, since our soul provides us with an example of it. But in the reasonable soul this representation is accompanied by consciousness, and it is then that it is called thought.'[20] In other words, consciousness transforms perception into thought. Leibniz is a reductionist in his treatment of the actions and passions of the soul. All states of the soul are perceptions. Actions are distinct perceptions; passions are confused perceptions. Moreover, appetite and perception are not two different things but only the same thing viewed in two different ways. When a present state is looked at as following upon the previous state it is called a perception; when it is looked at as giving rise to the succeeding or future state it is called an appetition. As for thought it is a perception of which we are conscious, while volition is an appetite of which we are conscious. Hence even thought and volition are the same thing viewed differently. Descartes, on the other hand, is not a reductionist. The different modes of thought are distinct kinds of actions or passions. They do not, however, form a heterogeneous collection of things, whose only common denominator is that we happen to be conscious of them. Doubting, affirming, desiring, imagining, perceiving, feelings are called

[19] *An Essay concerning Human Understanding*, II, i, 12.
[20] To Arnauld, 9 October 1687, *Die philosophischen Schriften von Gottfried Wilhelm Leibniz*, ed. C. I. Gerhardt, II, 112.

modes of thought by Descartes because 'they cannot be conceived apart from . . . an intelligent substance in which they reside, for . . . in their formal concept some kind of intellection is comprised.'[21] By this he does not mean that they are species of intellection, but that in the language of the *Principles* they 'presuppose' intellection. For example, imagining a triangle is quite distinct from conceiving a triangle, but is impossible without the prior conception of a triangle. 'This mode of thinking (i.e. imagining) differs from pure intellection only inasmuch as mind in its intellectual activity in some manner turns on itself, and considers some of the ideas which it possesses in itself; while in imagining it turns towards the body, and there beholds in it something conformable to the idea which it has either conceived of itself or perceived by the senses.'[22] However, even to see a triangle drawn on paper is to *recognize* a triangle, i.e. to see something conformable to an idea already possessed by the mind.[23] There is no need to recapitulate Descartes's account of the perception of the piece of wax in *Meditation* II, or the perception of the size, distance, and shape of objects in the *Dioptrics*, to emphasize this point that all sense perception of objects presupposes intellection. What, however, about the awareness of what in modern terms might be called a pure sense-datum, as when, for example, Descartes says, 'I see light, I hear noise, I feel heat'? What intellection is involved here? If we may go by the account given in the *Passions of the Soul*, we never have a feeling which is not situated *somewhere*. I feel joy or anger in the soul. I feel pain in the leg. I feel coldness in my hand, but warmth in the flame. I feel at the same time warmth in my hand but cold in the air. This necessary relating of feelings in one of three ways,—to my own body, to an external body, or to the soul—is, according to Descartes, a judgment; and it would appear then that there is no such thing in experience as a pure sense datum or feeling datum in isolation from a judgment. All judging involves conception—in the cases under consideration, conceptions of our bodies, of external bodies, or of our soul. Such common expressions as 'I see light, I hear noise, I feel pain', are all elliptical. Descartes maintains that it is only in our judgments

---

[21] *Meditation* VI. AT VII, 79. HR I, 190.
[22] Ibid. AT VII, 73. HR I, 186.
[23] *Reply* V. AT VII, 382. HR II, 228.

that we can err. We can be mistaken with regard to perceptions which we relate to our body, e.g. I may feel pain in a leg which has been amputated, and I may be mistaken with regard to those which we relate to external bodies, though we cannot, he says be mistaken with regard to those which we relate to the soul, 'inasmuch as they are so close to, and so entirely within our own soul, that it is impossible to feel them, without their being such as we feel them to be.'[24] That there is a pain in my leg may be false, but that I, an amputee, feel pain in my leg is certain, just as that the world is flat may be false, while that I judge that the world is flat can be certain. It may well, however, be questioned in passing whether relating joy and sorrow to the soul can, for Descartes, be a judgment any more than relating doubt to the soul is for him a judgement. But even if feeling joy or sorrow in the soul is not a judgment, nevertheless intellection is an essential element in all the passions, for the six primitive passions, of which all the others are composed or are species, namely, wonder, love, hatred, desire, joy, and sadness, have objects and thus presuppose conceptions of these objects. As such they are modes of thought.

Descartes' thesis that there are no perceptions, appetites, emotions, or sensations of which we are not conscious, can be seen to rest on two premises. The first is that there is no *intellection* of which we are not conscious. This is absolutely assumed. Here Leibniz goes beyond Descartes, and makes consciousness a condition of the very possibility of intellection or rationality. The second premise is that all perceptions, appetites, emotions, and sensations involve intellection. It follows that they must all fall within the orbit of consciousness. It is this second premise which Leibniz disputes. But here one is tempted to invoke against Leibniz Kant's dictum that percepts without concepts are blind. Blind perceptions are not perceptions at all. But more can be said on Descartes' side of the issue after we have considered the third element in his conception of the relation of thought and consciousness, namely that being conscious of what is occurring in the mind is not the same as thinking of what is occurring in the mind.

First, however, we must take note of a direct statement to the contrary in the *Conversation with Burman* on the question whether

[24] *Passions of the Soul*, I, xxvi. AT XI, 348. HR I, 343.

there can be anything in our mind, in so far as it is a thinking thing, of which it is not conscious. Burman raises the objection: 'But in what way could you be conscious, since to be conscious is to think? To think that you are conscious, you go on to another thought, and thus you are no longer thinking of what you were thinking previously, and thus you are not conscious of thinking, but of having thought,' To this Descartes replies, 'To be conscious is certainly to think, and to reflect on one's thought, but that this cannot occur so long as the previous thought remains, is false, because, as we have already seen, the soul can think several things at the same time, persevere in its thought, and whenever it pleases reflect on its thought, and thus be conscious of its thought.'[25] It must be observed that in this passage, in which to be conscious, to think about thought, and to reflect on thought, are all the same thing, thought is not something of which we are *always* conscious. Rather Descartes is saying here that we can reflect on our thought, or become conscious of our thought whenever it pleases us to do so. This is very different from the statement to Arnauld in *Replies IV* that 'There can exist in us no thought, of which at the very moment that is present to it, we are not conscious.' Because I can never think at any time without being conscious of my thought, but can at pleasure reflect upon or think about my thought, consciousness and reflection must be distinguished in Descartes and indeed the distinction is of great importance in Descartes' defence of his claim for the completely primitive nature of the *cogito ergo sum*. He has to contend with two criticisms, first, that prior to the *cogito ergo sum* he would have to know what thought and existence are, and second, that *I exist* is the conclusion of a syllogism whose premisses are, *he who thinks exists*, and *I think*. The major premiss must be know prior to the *cogito ergo sum*. As remarked in the previous paper on 'Innate Ideas',[26] the priority for Descartes of the knowledge of 'thought' and 'existence' to the enunciated proposition 'I think, therefore I am' in the priority of 'that internal cognition which always precedes reflective knowledge,' while the relation of the general proposition, 'he who thinks exists,' to 'I think, therefore I exist,' is one between what is known implicitly and what is known explicitly. We have implicit knowledge of everything present to consciousness, and any part of this implicit knowledge can be rendered explicit by the direction of attention upon it. In defining clear and distinct perception Descartes says, 'I term that clear which is present and apparent to an attentive mind . . . But the distinct is that which is so precise and different from all other objects that it contains nothing within itself but what is clear'.[27] Explicit knowledge, that which we get from attending to what we are conscious of as being in ourselves is, then, the *clear and distinct perception* of what we are pre-reflectively conscious of. Error can arise, according to Descartes, only when we allow ourselves to assent to what is not clearly and distinctly perceived. Accordingly, it follows that we *can* be mistaken about what is occurring in the mind, in spite of the fact that there is nothing in the mind of which the mind is not conscious. Moreover we can be ignorant or partially ignorant of what is in the mind in so far as ignorance is identified with lack of explicit knowledge. Thus Descartes can say that many men are ignorant of their beliefs. 'For since', he says, 'the act of thought by which we believe a thing is different from that by which we know that we believe it, the one often exists without the other.'[28] That act of thought by which we know that we believe, to which Descartes here refers, is the act of *attending* to our belief, so that we clearly and distinctly perceive what it is, although prior to any such attention we are conscious of our belief or have an implicit knowledge of it. And Descartes can also say that 'those who are most agitated by their passions are not those who know them best.' Powerful emotions are inimical to that careful attention and scrutiny which is necessary for the explicit knowledge of them, though we are nonetheless perfectly conscious of them.

The original statement that consciousness appears to demarcate an area of absolute certainty for Descartes must be amended in the following way. It demarcates an area of what is capable of being known with absolute certainty and of being exempted from hyperbolical doubt, provided we attend to what we are conscious of as existing in us. But if we all were in fact certain, or did in fact possess the explicit knowledge of what is in us, there would have been no need for Descartes to have pursued his *Meditations*, or to have published them.

[27] *Principles* I, xlv. AT VIII, 22. HR I, 237.
[28] *Discourse on Method.* AT VI, 23. HR I, 95.

To return now to Leibniz's criticism. Leibniz's argument for the existence of perceptions of which we are not conscious is based on a consideration of the nature of attention. The relevance of this consideration lies in the fact that Leibniz identifies consciousness or apperception with reflection upon, or attention to, what is in us, as Descartes does not. He says, 'There are a thousand indications which make us judge that there are at every moment an infinity of *perceptions* in us, but without apperception and reflection, i.e. changes in the soul itself of which we are not conscious, because the impressions are either too slight and too great in number, or too even, so that they have nothing sufficiently distinguishing them from each other; but joined to others they do produce their effect and to make themselves felt at least confusedly in the mass. Thus it is that habit makes us take no notice of the motion of a mill or a waterfall when we have lived quite near it for some time. It is not that the motion does not always strike our organs, and that something no longer enters the soul corresponding thereto, in virtue of the harmony of the soul and the body, but these impressions which are in the soul and the body, being destitute of the attractions of novelty, are not strong enough to attract our attention and our memory, attached to objects more engrossing. For all attention requires memory, and often when we are not admonished, so to speak, and warned to take notice of some of our own present perceptions, we allow them to pass without reflection, and even without being noticed; but if anyone directs our attention to them immediately afterwards, and makes us notice, for example, some noise which was just heard, we remember it, and are conscious of having had at the time some feeling of it. Thus there were perceptions of which we were not conscious at once, consciousness arising in this case only from the warning after some interval, however, small it may be.'[29]

Over the psychology of attention itself there may be little in what Leibniz says that Descartes would need to dispute, although Leibniz is mainly concerned with the conditions under which attention is captured, whereas Descartes is concerned with attention as deliberately focussed, the directing of attention being a principal element in his conception of method. The real issue separating the two philosophers is whether attention to what is

[29] *New Essays Concerning Human Understanding*, Preface. tr. A. G. Langley, Chicago (1916) 47f.

in us draws something up out of a subsconscious part of the mind, as Leibniz maintains, or whether what is in us is already there to consciousness for attention to be focussed on it, as Descartes maintains, On this point Descartes would appear to be the sounder psychologist. If something is out of sight in a subconscious, no amount of attention can perform the miracle of bringing it into view. Attention is not a light beam. It does not illuminate an object. It is possible only if the object is already in the light.

IV

'COGITO ERGO SUM':
INFERENCE OR ARGUMENT?

André Gombay

Consider what one Cartesian scholar has recently written about the *Cogito* and *Meditation Two*:

> It seems clear to me . . . that . . . Descartes regards his existence as something inferred. The purpose of the inference, however, is not to prove that *sum* is true . . . Descartes's concern is not to decide whether or not he exists, or to offer a proof of *sum*, but to establish that his existence is in a rather unusual sense certain or indubitable.[1]

This text contains three theses, of which I shall single out the first for examination:

(1) Descartes regards his existence as something inferred.
(2) The purpose of the inference is not to prove that '*sum*' is true;
(3) Descartes' concern is to establish that his existence is, in a rather unusual sense of 'indubitable', indubitable.

My question is this: is it true, as Frankfurt asserts, that Descartes regards his existence as something inferred?

It seems to me that we cannot begin to answer until we know a little more clearly exactly what is being asserted. What is it, to regard a state of affairs as *something inferred*? How does this differ from regarding it as not inferred, or from not regarding it as inferred? It is these words—'infer', 'inference'—to which I want to draw your attention.

Consider them for a moment as they might occur in one non-philosophical context. I say: 'When General De Gaulle flew precipitously to Germany last May, it was to make a bargain with the French generals: in exchange for their support in putting

---

[1] H. G. Frankfurt: 'Descartes' Discussion of his Existence in the Second Meditation', *Philosophical Review*, 1966, p. 333.

down a possible uprising in France, he agreed to an amnesty for the Algerian diehards'. You reply: 'This is all very well, but do you know for sure or is this mere inference on your part?'. This, I believe, is an entirely natural setting for the occurrence of the substantive 'inference', and also the verb 'to infer' (for you might have asked instead: 'Do you know for sure, or are you merely inferring?'). And it seems to me worthwhile to examine some of the features of *this* use of these words.

One fact is plain, of little philosophical interest, and I mention it first merely to get it out of the way. Plainly, in my example, inference is contrasted with knowledge, or at any rate first-hand knowledge. To concede that I infer is to concede that I do not really know. But plainly also, when Cartesian scholars worry about whether or not Descartes' *Cogito* is an inference, *this* contrast is not what they have in mind: whatever it comes to, the claim that Descartes regards his existence as something inferred is certainly not the claim that he regards his existence as something of which he is not really assured. What is more, even in my colloquial setting, this contrast is only one among several. Confronted with my assertion about De Gaulle and the generals, you might have asked: 'Is this something which you actually infer, or is it just a hunch, or an intuition?'; and here inference is set against guessing, or having an intuition (though of course not 'intuition' in the Cartesian sense, whatever that may be). For the purpose of understanding the debate about the *Cogito*, none of these contrasts is of any interest.

I now come to a second point, more important. That De Gaulle made a certain bargain with the French generals may be an inference on my part, without any inference on my part ever taking place. It may be something that I am inferring, and yet not be anything which I have inferred or about which it will be correct to say tomorrow that I inferred it yesterday. More generally: it is possible to speak of inference on my part without saying, or implying, that in my mind an inference took place. Rather, it is a matter of what I am now prepared, or in a position to do. If I assert P and P is an inference, I must be prepared to support my assertion with argument, to offer evidence; this evidence, however, is not first-hand or absolutely conclusive. No, I was not present when the agreement was being struck; and I have not received the confidences of any witness or participant.

Yet, soon after May 29th, General Massu's tanks came for 'manoeuvres' to the outskirts of Paris; and a few days later, General Salan was set free, and Georges Bidault returned from exile unprosecuted. The evidence may not be incontrovertible, but it is not easily dismissed. Notice that inferences, in this setting of the word, are not normally called *valid* or *invalid*: they are shaky, far-fetched, wild—when disparaged; reasonable, secure, irresistible—when approved. They are such, according to the strength of the evidence presented, or about to be presented.

My first thesis, then, is this: there exist settings where one can speak of an inference on someone's part without speaking about anything which is an event in that person's mental history. What I am inferring today I may also be inferring tomorrow; but it does not follow that I have inferred twice, or that it will be true tomorrow that I inferred yesterday. In speaking of inference, one is sometimes not speaking about anything that *takes place* in a mind.

But at other times, one is. Let me alter my example slightly. I am a close observer of the French political scene. On May 29th, I learn that De Gaulle is leaving Paris. A few hours later, a friend telephones from Colombey-les-deux-Eglises: the General has not arrived there. I then learn that the presidential limousine headed North, not East, from the Elysée; also, that at about the same time a helicopter from the Rhine Army landed in a remote corner of Le Bourget airfield, and it later took off amid great security precautions. It does not take me long to infer that De Gaulle has secretly flown to Germany. In speaking of inference here, I certainly seem to be speaking about something which took place in a mind, about a piece of reasoning. This is mental autobiography. Notice that in this setting, the verb 'to infer' is tensed, or at least it has a past, a perfect and a future tense. I might say: 'I promptly inferred (or 'drew the conclusion') that De Gaulle had left for Germany; so I rushed to the telephone and . . .' Anticipatorily, De Gaulle may have said: 'they will doubtless infer that I have gone to Colombey; however . . .' Notice also that people may infer wrongly.

It looks, then, as though inference is at least two things: sometimes it is a dated event or achievement in the mental history of a person, and sometimes it is not. I shall further conjecture that the distinction between dated and undated corresponds to a hiatus to be found in the tenses of the verb 'to infer': on one side we have past, perfect and future; on the other, present and continuous.

Now, about *tensed* inference (as I shall henceforth call it) there is one further point worth noticing. It is not customary to speak of 'having inferred', of 'having drawn a conclusion', where the matter is simple: that is, where the set of considerations present to the mind of a person who enunciates a conclusion falls below a certain level of complexity. It would be pompous on my part to say the following: 'I went to Colombey; saw that De Gaulle was not there; and so inferred that he was somewhere else'. It is quite true, of course, that I came to know that De Gaulle was elsewhere by finding out that he was not at Colombey; and therefore that my thought that he was elsewhere was, so to speak, the outcome of this other thought, the realisation that he was not at Colombey. Yet *this* fact is not sufficient warrant for my being said to have drawn a conclusion, or made an inference. At the same time, I can readily imagine myself saying: 'All right, De Gaulle is not here, so he is elsewhere'. More generally: there are situations where it is perfectly appropiate to say 'P so Q', but where it is inappropriate, or at any rate surprising, to be described as having inferred that Q, or drawn the conclusion that Q, or reasoned from P to Q. These last descriptions are naturally applicable only in circumstances where a person has, as the saying goes, to put two and two together, where at least a moderately large number of facts needs to be marshalled, where a modicum of ingenuity is required. In my coming to know that De Gaulle flew to Germany, these elements were present; in my coming to know that he was elsewhere than at Colombey, they were not.

My second thesis, then, is this: it is not colloquially appropriate to speak of a person making an inference in every situation where that person offers an argument. The importance of this point for understanding Descartes will, I hope, emerge soon.

For the moment, however, I return to my last example. I go to Colombey, fail to find De Gaulle, and say: 'De Gaulle is not here; so he is elsewhere'. This, I have just claimed, is, with most men, something too simple to be called *inference* (in the common use of that word). But suppose now that an astute logician should reply: 'But really, this is not simple at all. For there is a further proposition involved, namely this: "At every moment everybody is somewhere". So why hold that no "inference" has occurred?'. What are we to make of this objection?

It seems to me that we can offer at least this reply: that when *I* (in the example) said 'De Gaulle is not here, so he is elsewhere', the thought of the proposition 'At every moment everybody is somewhere' did not cross my mind. It could have crossed, but it didn't. Insofar as we allow to people the ability sometimes to report correctly what goes through their minds when they say what they say, there seems to be no reason why my report of what went on, on this occasion, should not be accepted. As a matter of fact, there might be very good inductive evidence to support a claim such as mine: the majority of mankind is probably well capable of offering an argument of the form '*A* is not here, so *A* is elsewhere', yet most probably *in*capable of having, let alone formulating, the thought expressed in the sentence 'At every moment everybody is somewhere'. So the argument can doubtless occur without the thought.

At this point, the objector will probably reply that I am cheating, that I have deliberately misrepresented the claim that, in 'De Gaulle is not here, so he is elsewhere', the conclusion depends on the further premiss 'At every moment everybody is somewhere'. Well, whether I am cheating or not depends on what the objector himself means by 'depends'. If his claim was that the thought of the premiss must in *some* fashion (perhaps 'implicitly') be present in the mind of any person who offers the argument, then my reply is perfectly in order. The premiss is *not* involved in the argument, if 'being involved' means that its thought is a necessary episode in the mental history of anyone by whom the argument is propounded.

But then, the objector probably meant something else. The likelihood is that he was talking not about inference (in any sense of 'inference' encountered so far), but about what logicians call *argument*. And this is something quite different.

In logicians' language, to offer an argument is—typically—to say something of the form '$P_1, P_2, \ldots, P_n$, so Q'; and most of the time there is only one P. The occurrence of some such set of sentences is a *prima facie* sufficient condition for the occurrence of an argument. So much seems plain enough. Notice however, that in actual life arguments (in the logicians' sense) can come to be uttered in basically two distinct types of settings. Suppose I say to my wife: 'I want to take the dog out tonight before dinner, so I must be home no later than 8'. What I have done here is first to state a certain fact, that I wish to take the dog out before dinner, and then spell out a certain consequence of the fact. But the same argument could have occurred, so to speak, from the other end. I might have said to my wife: 'I must be home no later than 8 tonight'; and perhaps she replied: 'Why? Dinner will not be as early as that'; and I reply: 'Ah yes, but I want to take the dog out tonight before dinner, so I must be home no later than 8'. Here, the situation is different. I first utter my (eventual) conclusion; am queried; so offer the (eventual) premiss in support. Basically, then, arguments occur in these two ways in actual discourse; they can be propounded from the premiss, as a spelling out of alleged consequences, or they can be propounded for the conclusion, as a means of providing support.

It is perhaps worth reminding ourselves that we have here a semi-technical use of a word: in neither of my settings would I normally be described as having offered an *argument*. In the second, for instance, I might be said to have offered an explanation. Still, although not colloquial, the logicians' use is I think not obscure.

An argument, then, occurs whenever anything of the form 'P, so Q' occurs, in thought, speech or print, and when these words can be readily construed either as the putative spelling out of a consequence of P or as the putative provision of support for Q. Further, it makes sense, I think, to speak of the *purpose* of an argument only if by 'argument' we mean argument as it occurs in the second of these ways, as the provision of support. And it makes sense to speak, as Frankfurt does, of the purpose of an *inference* only if by 'inference' we mean argument. There does of course exist such a use of that word, though it is one, I believe, largely confined to philosophers.

There is one plain difference, which comes out in the grammar, between offering an argument and (tensedly) inferring: an argument is something offered *by* A *to* B, an inference is something made *by* A. In this sense, I shall say that arguments are *public* and inferences *private*. To say this is of course not to deny that, sometimes, one argues to oneself and conducts the argument just in one's head; but this does not turn the argument into an inference. That is a matter not of psychology, but of the description of what takes place. It is also worth noticing that, unlike 'infer', the verb 'to offer an argument' conjugates smoothly throughout its tenses.

Let me now, and for the last time, return to my 'De Gaulle is not here, so he is elsewhere', and to the objection that the premiss 'At every moment everybody is somewhere' is involved in the argument. In a fiercely obstinate and contrary mood, I might still refuse to concede. I might reply: 'Well, the premiss was not in *my* argument; I never uttered any such words'. But this move, one feels, would not carry me very far. For it invites the reply: 'Perhaps the premiss was not present in *your* argument; however, it is involved in *the* argument'. Or better still: 'The premiss may not actually have been in, but it is *implicit in*, your argument; for your conclusion depends on it'. And here I should have to concede.

My last obstinate reply had perhaps one merit: it helped to bring out the fact that argument—like tenseless, but unlike tensed, inference—leads a double life. On the one hand, it is something personal, the propounder's words; but it is also something which is no-one's property and is shared by all rational beings. In this fashion, one can speak of a premiss *implicit in* an argument: not to mean that the thought of such a premiss is in some manner present in the mind of anyone by whom the argument is propounded, or that it exists as a mental capacity of which each propounding is an actualisation, but rather that this premiss is the logically weakest proposition required in addition to the existing premisses in order to turn the argument into one which is deductively valid. So when my objector insists that the premiss 'At every moment everybody is somewhere' *is* involved, he means that a sentence stating at least that proposition would have to be uttered in addition to 'De Gaulle is here' if one wanted to provide conclusive, or entailing, support for the utterance of 'De Gaulle is elsewhere'. And of course he is right.

For convenience, I shall now introduce a piece of jargon: I shall say that my first two replies to the objector ((a): 'The thought never crossed my mind'; (b): 'The words never crossed my lips') are replies in the *personal mode*; and my third (conceding the objection) a reply in the *impersonal*.

So finally, let us turn to Descartes. Perhaps you have sensed a certain affinity between the question involving De Gaulle and Colombey with which I have been concerned, and the philosophers' debate about whether the *Cogito* is, or is not, an inference. I have delayed looking at the *Cogito* because I hold that the distinctions which have been drawn so far are the ones required for settling this debate; and there is everything to be gained from drawing them in an atmosphere less paralysing than that of the *Cogito* itself. For here, the reader is paralysed, or at least inhibited, by a double uncertainty: what does '*cogito*' mean?; what can '*sum*' possibly mean? With these substantial problems, I shall not in any manner be concerned.

About the *Cogito*, two facts at least are plain: first, that the words '*cogito ergo sum*' do not occur anywhere in the *Meditations*; secondly, that there is one thesis put forward in the third paragraph of *Meditation Two* which Descartes, throughout his life, regarded as correctly expressed by the words '*cogito ergo sum*'. To my knowledge, nowhere does Descartes disown the formula or declare it in any way misleading.

Here are the last lines of that paragraph:

> But I have convinced myself that nothing in the world exists—no sky, no earth, no minds, no bodies; so have I not also convinced myself that I do not exist?' No: if I did convince myself of anything [here the French adds: 'or if I merely thought of anything'], I must have existed. 'But there is some deceiver, supremely powerful, supremely intelligent, who purposely always deceived me.' If he deceives me, then again I undoubtedly exist; let him deceive me as much as he may, he will never bring it about that, at the time of thinking that I am something, I am in fact nothing. Thus I have now weighed all considerations enough and more than enough; and must at length conclude (*statuendum sit*) that this proposition 'I am', 'I exist', whenever I utter it or conceive it in my mind, is necessarily true.[2]

When the words 'I am', 'I exist' occur in the last sentence of this text, it is undeniable that they occur as the conclusion of at least one argument. First Descartes observes that he has con-

[2] On the whole, the translation is that of Elizabeth Anscombe and Peter Thomas Geach in *Descartes: Philosophical Writings* (London, 1954), p. 67. Henceforth, 'AG'.

vinced himself of a number of things. He then wonders whether he has also convinced himself that he does not exist. And he replies that he hasn't, for he exists if he has convinced himself of anything. Schematically, it goes like this:

> Observation: P (= 'I have convinced myself of some things')
> Question: Have I convinced myself that not-Q (= 'that I do not exist')?
> Answer: No; for Q, if P.

Clearly, this is an argument, offered in support of its conclusion. It deviates, however, in two—perhaps related—respects from the standard pattern: (a) Descartes is soliloquising, so propounder and recipient are one and the same; (b) the conclusion comes to be entertained through its being asked whether a certain proposition, incompatible with that conclusion, is true. These look like minor deviations. But as we shall see later on, it may well be that Descartes thought them important.

So one point has now been conclusively, and indeed very easily, settled: in the first five lines of the third paragraph of *Meditation Two* there is one argument whose conclusion is *'sum'* and whose premiss, adduced in support of that conclusion, is recognisably like *'cogito'*. Why then, one may ask, has there ever been a debate about whether Descartes himself regarded the *Cogito* as an inference?

There has been, because of Descartes' peculiar answers to one objection with which he was confronted. Here is the objection, as reported by Descartes himself:

> . . . The author of the Rejoinders [Gassendi] will have it that when I say *I think therefore I am*, I am presupposing the major premiss: *what thinks, is*, and have thus already embraced a prejudice.

This is Descartes' *Letter* to Clerselier (Jan. 1646) (AG 299-300). It is not difficult to make out in a general way what the objection comes to: Descartes is being accused of inconsistency. If it is possible that an evil genius deceives Descartes even in those matters which Descartes thinks he knows perfectly well, then it is possible that the proposition 'whatever thinks, is' is false. But this proposition is involved in 'I think therefore I am'. So it is possible that the conclusion 'I am' is false. Yet in *Meditation Two*

Descartes had claimed that 'I am' is necessarily true whenever he utters it or conceives it in his mind. Hence, the inconsistency. In short then, the objection is that, if the hypothesis of the evil genius is taken seriously, Descartes is not entitled to assert, as he does in *Meditation Two*: 'I am, I exist'. This objection preoccupied Descartes, and he repeatedly sought to meet it.

Basically, he offers what look like two lines of reply. The first appears for the first time in a well known, and lately much discussed, passage, in the *Reply* to the *Second Set of Objections* (AG. 299):

> . . . When we observe that we are thinking beings, this is a sort of primary notion, which is not the conclusion of any syllogism; and, moreover, when somebody says: *I think, therefore I am, or exist,* he is not syllogistically deducing his existence from a thought, but recognising it as something self-evident, in a simple mental intuition. This is clear from the fact that if he were deducing it syllogistically he would first have to know the major premise: *whatever thinks is or exists*; whereas really it is rather that this principle is learnt through his observing in his own case the impossibility of having a thought without existing. For our mind is so constituted as to form general propositions from knowledge of particular cases.

In this *Reply*, two points stand out:
(1) The answer appears to be entirely in the personal mode; that is, in terms of what does, and what does not, go on in the mind of someone who says 'I think therefore I am'; and Descartes denies—perhaps reasonably—that the thought 'Whatever thinks, is or exists' must occur. More questionably, he couples this denial with a general theory of how thoughts of this kind come to be entertained. So that the answer is perhaps not in terms of the history of one mind, but in terms of the constitution of the mind.
(2) A certain contrast is drawn, but it is not one between argument and intuition. What Descartes denies—perhaps again quite reasonably—is that anything like a process of reasoning must take place when a man says 'I think therefore I am'; and a similar denial could, as we saw, be made in the case of 'De Gaulle is not here so he is elsewhere'. But to deny this is not tantamount to denying that the words constitute an *argument*. On this point, the

French version is even more explicit than the Latin. For here, the end of the first sentence reads like this:

> . . . when somebody says: *I think therefore I am, or exist,* his existing is a self-evident conclusion from his thinking, and not one drawn *via* a syllogism; it is seen by simple mental intuition.

Here, we do not find, as in the Latin, even the possible suggestion of a contrast between (a) concluding and (b) recognising as self-evident: here, 'I am' is squarely called a *conclusion.* What is contrasted is (a) coming to a conclusion by syllogism and (b) coming to a conclusion by simple mental intuition. And incidentally, 'simple mental intuition' would not be out of place as the description of what normally takes place in the mind of a man who says 'De Gaulle is not here, so he is elsewhere': simple mental intuition, because reasoning is not required.

Such, then, is Descartes' first line of defence. It is deployed in 1641, in the *Reply* which we have just been considering; and again in 1646, in the *Letter* to Clerselier, which contains Gassendi's objection (AG. 300):

> . . . But the most important mistake here is that the author supposes that the knowledge of particular propositions must be deduced from universal ones, following the syllogistic order of Dialectic. This shows how little he knows the right way of seeking for truth; for in order to discover the truth one must assuredly begin with particular notions, and then go on to general ones afterwards; although, conversely, after having discovered the general notions, one can likewise deduce further particular notions from them. For example, when a child is taught the elements of geometry, he cannot be made to understand in general that *if from equal quantities equal parts are subtracted the remainders are still equal* or that *the whole is greater than its parts,* unless he is shown examples in particular cases. It is from ignoring this that our author has been misled into so many fallacious reasonings, with which he has swelled his volume; he has simply made up false major premises out of his own imagination, as though I had deduced from these the truths I explained.

Here, especially in the last sentence, we have again the answer in the personal mode; and again conjoined with a theory about how knowledge of certain kinds of propositions is generally acquired.

This defence is also deployed in the *Conversation* with Burman, in 1648 (I deliberately quote here only part of the text; the omitted sentences will be supplied later):

> Before reaching this conclusion *I think therefore I am*, one can have knowledge of the major premiss *whatever thinks, is* . . . .
> . . . .
> But I have a prior knowledge of my conclusion in that I attend only to what I experience in myself, i.e. to *I think therefore I am*, while not likewise attending the general principle, *whatever thinks is*. As I have pointed out, we do not in fact separate these general propositions from particular cases but rather take notice of them in the particulars.

Together with this line of defence goes Descartes' insistence on the simplicity of the *Cogito*. In a *Letter* to Colvius (1640), Descartes writes of 'I think therefore I am' that 'it is something so simple, and so natural to infer, that it might have come from the pen of anyone'. And in 1648, in a *Letter* to the Marquess of Newcastle (AG. 300-301), he describes the *Cogito* as something which is not a 'product of reasoning', but something which 'the mind sees, feels, handles'. Once again, however, to insist on this point is not to deny that the *Cogito* is an argument.

So much for one line of reply. But there is in Descartes yet another. It consists in his conceding that the disputed major premiss *is* involved in the argument, but in claiming that this premiss is not one whose truth is rendered doubtful by the hypothesis of the evil genius. This thesis is stated—incorrectly —in the *Principles* (I, 10) (AG. 183-184):

> When I said that the proposition *I think therefore I am* is the first and the most certain of those we come across when we philosophise in an orderly way, I was not denying that we must first know what is meant by *thinking, existence, certainty*; and again we must know such things as that *it is impossible for that which is thinking to be non-existent*; but I thought it needless to enumerate these notions, for they are of the greatest simplicity, and by themselves they can give us no knowledge that anything exists.

Now this text certainly seems at odds with the *Reply* to the *Second Set of Objections*, and Descartes was questioned about this by

Burman. He offered the following exegesis—and these are the sentences omitted from my earlier quotation of the *Conversation:*

> Before reaching this conclusion *I think therefore I am,* one can have knowledge of the major premise *whatever thinks, is,* because it is in reality prior to my conclusion, and my conclusion depends on it. And this is the sense in which, in the *Principles,* the author says it precedes the conclusion, since implicitly it is always presupposed and prior. But I do not always have an explicit knowledge of its priority.

If this is what Descartes meant in the *Principles,* he certainly put it very badly there.[3] But exactly what did he mean? In the *Conversation* he speaks of the dependence of the *Cogito* upon, and of the priority relatively to the *Cogito* of, the premiss 'whatever thinks, is'. It seems to me entirely reasonable to interpret Descartes as in effect offering here my impersonal answer to the De Gaulle-argument objector; that is, as in effect saying that the proposition 'whatever thinks, is' is required in addition to 'I think' to complete a set of propositions which would constitute entailing support for the assertion of 'I am'. It is in this sense that the contested proposition is 'implicitly presupposed' and 'prior'.

Such is, I think, the thought which Descartes intended to convey in *Principles I, 10,* concerning the *Cogito* and 'whatever thinks, is'; and in the article immediately following, he goes on to claim that the premiss is known by the natural light, *i.e.* that it is not of a kind to be made doubtful by the possible existence of an evil genius.

So we find, or seem to find, in Descartes two main answers to the charge that he has 'embraced a prejudice'. In one mood, Descartes *denies* that the proposition 'whatever thinks, is' is involved in the *Cogito*; and these are the more numerous texts. Here, Descartes is speaking about what occurs in people's heads, or at least in his head; and he denies that the thought of a certain proposition occurs. On the other hand, and in another mood, he sometimes *concedes* that 'whatever thinks, is' is involved in the *Cogito,* but asserts that it is a premiss to which he is entitled, the

---

[3] It may look like dubious exegetical practice, on my part, to dismiss as inaccurate one text (the *Principles*) which Descartes wrote and had published, in the name of another (the *Conversation*), which is not from Descartes' pen, and whose accuracy he is not known to have checked. The practice is dubious. But here we are all clutching at straws.

G

doubt notwithstanding. Here, Descartes is speaking about the content not of a mind, but of an argument.

In short, then, we seem to have two theses:

(1) in *Meditation Two*, '*sum*' is not the conclusion of a piece of syllogistic reasoning, because no reasoning is required for asserting '*cogito ergo sum*'. Taken in the personal mode, the *Cogito* is not a syllogistic argument.

(2) However, the *Cogito* is a syllogistic argument, if taken impersonally: in '*cogito ergo sum*', the premiss '*illud omne, quod cogitat, est*' is implicitly presupposed.

As I have argued, these two theses are not in any way incompatible: and when they are considered each by itself, they both look reasonable, or at least defensible.

But surely, they are not both defensible as answers to the charge with which Descartes was confronted. For when Gassendi accuses Descartes of 'having embraced a prejudice', the charge is hardly that, in the course of his meditations, Descartes came to entertain some unworthy thoughts; but rather that he came to assert what he was not entitled to assert. And this charge is hardly met by insisting, as Descartes does, that his mind is naturally so constituted as to entertain the thought of the *Cogito* without also entertaining the thought that whatever thinks is. If De Gaulle were to say 'I am a Frenchman, hence I am right', he would not I think be viewed as answering the charge of prejudice were he to declare that this particular truth is one which his mind 'sees, feels, handles', whereas the thought that all Frenchman are right was one which he had never entertained, his mind being so constituted as to 'not in fact separate such general propositions from particular cases, but rather take notice of them in the particulars'. It looks, then, as though Descartes is either confused or perverse: he is asked for entitlement, he offers personal history.

Yet it is unattractive to believe that Descartes could have been delinquent so patently and so grossly. Surely, one feels, he must have had a reason for persistently answering the objection in this way. And the question is: what reason?

The answer, I think, lies in a strange theory that Descartes seems to have held concerning the nature of *demonstration*, a theory which is put forward in the *Reply* to the *Second Set of Objections*, immediately before the so-called proof *more geometrico*.

Though the passage is rather long, I shall reproduce it in full:

> Demonstration is of two kinds, by analysis or by synthesis.
> Analysis shows the very manner in which the thing has been methodically discovered, so to speak *a priori*; so provided the reader follows, and keeps his mind on every point, he will understand what is demonstrated no less perfectly, and make it no less his own, than if he had discovered it himself. However, this kind of demonstration is not such as to compel assent in a reader who is inattentive or hostile; and if any point put forward is inadvertently passed over, the conclusion will no longer be seen as necessary. Also on many points which are clear enough in themselves, analysis will not expatiate, though they be precisely those which it is most important to keep in mind.
> Synthesis, on the other hand, proceeds in the reverse manner, so to speak *a posteriori* (though it may also contain proofs going the other way). It does indeed demonstrate its conclusions clearly, by using definitions, postulates, axioms, theorems and problems, so that if any single step is challenged, it may at once be shown to be contained in an earlier step; so the reader, however obstinate and stubborn, is compelled to assent. However, unlike analysis, this way of proving does not really satisfy those who are eager to learn, because it does not show in what manner the thing itself has been discovered.[4]

Although Descartes is here speaking about geometrical proof, it is clear that he does not intend the distinction between 'analysis' and 'synthesis' to apply only to geometry; for he immediately goes on to say that he himself has followed the 'analytic' method in the *Meditations*. Now, there is a good deal in this passage which I find exceedingly difficult to understand. But at least three general points seem assured:

(1) Descartes is contrasting two things, but they are *not* demonstration and discovery; they are two kinds of demonstration.

(2) To demonstrate P 'synthetically' is, *inter alia*, to offer entailing support for the assertion of P; in fact, it looks as though the Cartesian notion of 'synthesis' is roughly our informal notion of proof.

[4] An English translation of this passage is to be found in HR II, 48–49.

(3) Descartes holds that, for at least some P, there is a method of demonstrating P, which (a) shows how the demonstrator himself discovered P, and (b) makes the person to whom P is demonstrated in this fashion feel about P as though he had discovered it himself.

It seems to me that Descartes' surprising mode of answer to Gassendi begins to appear intelligible in the light of his belief in the existence of this powerful kind of demonstration, 'analysis'. For when he persists in replying in the personal mode, he is not unwittingly confusing argumentation and personal history; rather, he takes himself to be offering, or recalling, a proof, precisely by recounting what went on in his mind when he came to assert 'I think therefore I am'. The thought of the proposition 'Whatever thinks, is' did not occur; however, 'analytic' proof proceeds by displaying precisely what did occur; hence, that proposition is not part of one 'analytic' proof of 'I am'. Descartes' answer is not simple-minded autobiography, but autobiography *qua* demonstration.

To say that Descartes' procedure is intelligible in the light of a certain belief is however not to say that that belief is itself intelligible.   For my part, I cannot see that it is. We are told that the *Meditations* were written in the 'analytic' mode: plagiarising the first sentence of the *Tractatus Logico-Philosophicus*, we might construe Descartes as saying that the *Meditations* will be understood only by someone who feels as though he himself has had the thoughts which are expressed in them. Yet insofar as anything in the *Meditations* is recognisably a piece of argumentation—say the third paragraph of *Meditation Two*—it scarcely measures up to the general claims made in the *Reply* on behalf of the 'analytic' mode of proof. There is of course the quasi-historical setting, the narrative in the first person, the frequent self-addressed questions: but it is difficult to regard these as anything more than stylistic deviations from the pattern of proof which Descartes calls 'synthetic'. I do not deny that there might be ways of leading a person to see 'how things stand', which are not those of deductive demonstration; but I do not discern any of these anywhere in the *Meditations*; and I can conceive of none that might accomplish what 'analysis' is said to accomplish. In the *Reply*, Descartes opines that the ancient Geometers knew about 'analysis', but chose to present their proofs by 'synthesis' because they set such high value on the former that they wished to keep its existence secret. Alas, it has remained a secret.

———————

For all the opacity of the doctrine of argumentation on which they ultimately rest, Descartes' answers to the question of whether 'whatever thinks, is' is involved in the *Cogito* have two virtues which are not shared by the writings of other philosophers devoted to these answers.

One, Descartes makes it quite plain that, insofar as dependence on a further premiss is concerned, the case of the *Cogito* is by no means unique. Most clearly in the *Letter* to Clerselier, but elsewhere also, Descartes points out that 'whatever thinks, is' is but one of a class of truths which (a) are implicit in actually presented arguments, and yet (b) are such that they cannot be formulated, or even entertained, by the propounders of these arguments. What holds of 'I think therefore I am' also holds of—say—'Brittany is part of France, so France is larger than Brittany'; and it would also hold of 'De Gaulle is not here, so he is elsewhere' (provided that 'De Gaulle' is taken to stand for a certain union-of-mind-and-body). Where Descartes is at pains to point out that '*cogito ergo sum*' resembles countless other arguments in being something perceived by simple mental intuition, his modern commentators write as though precisely the opposite were the case: they devote immense attention to '*cogito*' and to '*sum*', but treat '*ergo*' as though it were something so transparent as to require no discussion. This is no trifling oversight: for in the end it is precisely his views about '*ergo*' which account for Descartes' position.

The second difference between Descartes and his modern commentators is this. Descartes' discussions of the *Cogito* and 'whatever thinks, is' take place in a well-defined setting: Descartes is defending himself against the charge that the *Cogito* rests on a premiss which he ought to have rejected. The modern discussions occur against the background of a different, and much vaguer, question: is the *Cogito* an inference, or is it something else? In one way, the question is not vague at all and admits of definite answers. *Is* the *Cogito* an inference? Well, if we mean: 'Is it tenseless inference (i.e. inference of the kind which I engage in when I assert without conclusive evidence that De Gaulle flew to make a bargain with the French generals)?', the answer is: 'Of course not'. If we mean: 'Is there anywhere a putative argument offered by Descartes of which the conclusion is "*sum*" and the premiss "*cogito*"?', the answer is: 'Yes, in the third paragraph of *Meditation Two*'. If we mean: 'Is the *Cogito* always the outcome of a piece of reasoning?', the answer is: 'No', if 'reasoning' is so used as to exclude cases of simple mental intuition: and 'Yes', otherwise. These answers are plain, decidable, and philosophically unexciting. Yet when we look at the writings of the modern commentators we find that, generally, they do not even take one step in the direction of these answers. The reason is that they are hunting for bigger game. They are struck by the non-straight-forward character of the *Cogito*'s premiss or conclusion, and it is these that they wish to investigate. It is of course highly desirable that '*cogito*' and '*sum*' should be, if they can be, adequately understood. But understanding them does not seem to be either a necessary or a sufficient condition of deciding whether the *Cogito* is an inference. It may well be, for instance, that the utterance of the grammatical contradictory of '*sum*' is in some unique fashon self-stultifying. But why should this be held to show that the *Cogito* is not an inference? On this point, some explanation is required.

One final remark. Commentators sometimes point out that in some places (*e.g.* his *Reply* to Father Bourdin—the 'basket of apples' passage, HR II, 282) Descartes writes, not '*cogito ergo sum*', but '*ego cogitans sum*'. *That*, in my view, holds exactly as much philosophical interest as the fact that, coming to Colombey, I might have said: 'Well, not being here, De Gaulle is elsewhere'.[5]

---

[5] I have learned much about the matters discussed here from Harry Frankfurt, Ian Hacking and Anthony Kenny.

V

DESCARTES' THEORY OF CLEAR AND DISTINCT IDEAS

E. J. ASHWORTH

It is widely agreed that Descartes took ideas to be the objects of knowledge and that his theory of clear and distinct ideas arose from his attempt to find a way of picking out those ideas whose truth was so certain and self-evident that the thinker could be said to know them with certainty. To say of an idea that it is clear and distinct was, he believed, to say of it both that it was certainly true and that any claim to know it was justified. No other criterion need be appealed to. It is at this point, however, that most of those who set out to expound Descartes' theory of knowledge are brought to a standstill. The part played by clear ideas is obvious enough, but what did Descartes mean by 'clear and distinct'? This paper is an attempt, not to make an original contribution to the study of Descartes, but to elucidate his terms and evaluate his criterion in the light of what both he and others have written. In order to avoid restating the whole of his philosophical system, I shall begin with a brief statement of my general assumptions about the nature of his endeavour.

Like most of his contemporaries, Descartes adopted a representative theory of sense perception by which ideas are a necessary intermediary between the mind and what is external to it, and he extended this theory to apply not only to sensory objects but to all external reality, including God and the eternal truths.[1] Since he believed that ideas were the only objects with which we were immediately acquainted, he felt that any theory about their external reference and the nature of their relationship with other realities had to be consequent upon a thorough examination of ideas and their properties. Our judgements must be in accordance with our ideas;[2] and our criteria must be criteria which are applicable to ideas. Since his chief interest was in establishing a

[1]AT III, 474.
[2]AT III, 476.

body of certain knowledge, his first task was to settle upon an idea which was known with certainty, so that he could formulate a criterion for picking out other such ideas or statements in the light of the evidence thus obtained.

He did claim that in a sense we already have a body of certain knowledge before we begin the search for an example, and he cited the cases of 'thought', 'doubt', 'certainty', 'truth', 'existence'.[3] These are indefinable, like a colour. All we can do is open our eyes and see, for words will never help us to grasp them. However, while we recognize what 'doubt' etc. are and must know them with certainty in order to be able to think at all, we cannot claim that these ideas give us knowledge of anything that actually exists.[4] Hence they afford us no starting place; they are merely necessary conditions for the making of a start. In this discussion Descartes seems to be suggesting that we have a series of special intuitions of processes and states; but his point could also be made in terms of an artificial language, in which a set of primitive symbols and syntactical rules must be adopted before anything can be said, whether in or about the language.

We can now see how Descartes came to pick out his first piece of certain knowledge, and to use it in the formulation of his criterion for knowledge. His own account of what he did is most misleading, for he says that it was as if he were separating good from rotten apples; he just turned them all out of the basket and put the good apples to one side.[5] Chisholm rightly remarks that this suggests that Descartes had a method of telling evident beliefs from non-evident beliefs even before he began;[6] but the criticism does not apply to the procedure of the *Meditations*. Here Descartes begins his search for the indubitable by doubting all propositions, and then looking to see whether he is led to an absurdity. If −p is clearly untenable, then p must be a piece of certain knowledge, and can be used as a paradigm case of knowledge. To deny that I exist while I doubt or think or deny is clearly absurd; hence "I think, therefore I exist" is our foundation stone, our first certain truth. When Descartes examines the nature of this statement, he finds that he has a clear and distinct perception of it, and concludes: "It seems to me that already I can establish

[3] HR I, 222, 325.
[4] HR I, 222.
[5] HR II, 282.
[6] R. Chisholm, *Perceiving* (Ithaca, N.Y., 1957), pp. 32–3.

as a general rule that all things which I perceive very clearly and distinctly are true."[7] Thus, he claims, he has discovered not only an example of certain knowledge, but a distinguishing mark of certain knowledge.

Descartes felt that some obvious difficulties still remained. So long as it is possible that an evil genius exists, we have a reason for doubting the general rule enunciated above, even if we are incapable of doubting particular instances of that rule. Moreover, the human mind is notoriously weak in its powers of attention, and can easily lose grip on those truths it has momentarily grasped.[8] But the proof that God exists dispelled both these difficulties, by removing any reason we might have for general doubt, and by furnishing us with a guarantee that what we remember having perceived clearly and distinctly is true. Fortunately the problems raised by the proofs for the existence of God, the so-called vicious circle, the distinction between general and particular doubt, and the nature of the *cogito* need not be discussed here; and I shall now turn to a more detailed examination of what Descartes had to say about ideas.

The fact that Descartes adopted the word 'idea' is itself significant. When scholastic philosophers discussed human cognition, they spoke of the mind as containing concepts (*species, intentiones*). They claimed that these concepts originated through our sense perceptions, and hence that they stood in some relation to external objects. The term 'concept' was contrasted with the term 'idea'. Ideas were the eternal essences or archetypes contemplated by God, and the question of their external reference did not arise. They were an integral part of God's mind. God could create instances of one of his ideas, but his idea was in no way dependent upon the existence of such instances. Descartes took the word 'idea' and applied it to the contents of the human mind because he wanted to escape the suggestion that these contents must be in some sense dependent on the external world as a causal agent.[9] He wished to establish the logical possibility that a mind and the ideas contained within it are unrelated to other existents, and can be discussed in isolation from them.

Descartes saw the term 'idea' as having a very wide extension.

---

[7] HR I, 158.
[8] AT IV, 116; HR I, 167, 183.
[9] HR II, 68.

He said " . . . I take the term idea to stand for whatever the mind directly perceives,"[10] where the verb 'perceive' refers to any possible cognitive activity, including sensing, imagining and conceiving.[11] Thus a sense datum, a memory, an image, and a concept can all be called ideas. This, of course, leads to the blurring of distinctions. For Descartes, "I have an idea of red" may mean that I am now sensing something red, or that I have a concept of the colour red, even if I am not now picking out an instance of that concept. Moreover, when Descartes speaks of an idea, he may be taking it as representative of some object or quality in the physical world, as when he says "I have an idea of the sky and stars," or he may be referring to the meaning he assigns to a word, as when he says "I have an idea of substance." Nor does he make any distinction between "having an idea" and "entertaining a proposition." Such statements as "Nothing comes from nothing" and "The three angles of a triangle are equal to two right angles" are categorized as 'common notions',[12] and are included among the contents of the mind. Descartes does remark that in some cases an idea may be expressed by a name, in other cases by a proposition,[13] but he does not bother to pursue this line of inquiry.

One of the characteristics of an idea is 'objective reality', a scholastic phrase which Descartes adopted, but used in a new way. In scholastic writings the terms 'subjective' and 'objective' have meanings which are the reverse of the modern meanings. An object like a table exists subjectively or as a subject if it has spatio-temporal existence, if it is real or actual. In contrast, the concept of a table can be looked at as having two kinds of existence. The concept *qua* concept has formal existence, but the concept as having some specifiable content is said to have objective existence, or existence as an object of thought. The concepts of a table and of a chair are formally similar but object-ively different. So far as subjective realities were concerned, the scholastics assigned them different grades of reality according to their perfection and causal power. For instance, a substance is more perfect and causally more efficacious than an accident, hence a man has a higher grade of reality than the colour red.

[10] HR II, 67–8.
[11] HR I, 232.
[12] HR I, 239.
[13] AT III, 395.

It was also held that every effect had a cause with either an equal or a higher grade of reality. These doctrines were not seen as having any relevance to concepts. As formally existent, a concept has of course to have some cause, but the content of the concept was not seen as having any independent reality. Descartes, however, felt that the objective reality could be considered independently of its formal reality, and that it must be graded just as subjective reality was graded. The idea of a man, he felt, has more objective reality than the idea of a colour. Moreover, the cause of the idea containing a certain degree of objective reality must have an equal or greater degree of subjective reality. For instance, the idea of God has so high a degree of objective reality that only God himself is perfect enough to be the cause of such an idea.[14]

In the same way as an idea can be characterized as possessing a certain degree of objective reality, it can be characterized as possessing a certain degree of truth. Sometimes Descartes treated the predicate 'true' as if it were synonymous with 'real'. He claimed that "truth consists in being and falsity in non-being;"[15] and it followed that an idea was more or less true as it had more or less being or objective reality. Our idea of the Infinite or God is entirely true, because its object is entirely real.[16] Descartes seems to have had in mind the mediaeval doctrine of transcendentals, by which the terms 'one', 'true', and 'good' are convertible with the term 'being'. However, he recognized that truth is not merely an intrinsic property of ideas, since it involves a relationship between an idea and an object, whether actual or possible. In one of his letters, he said that to call some proposition or idea true is to assert "a conformity between thought and object," and that if one refers to objects as being true, one means only that they can be the object of a true thought.[17] In another letter, he said that our clear ideas are true in the sense that their object does exist, if we see that it is not possible for it not to exist, and that their object may exist, if we see that its existence is possible.[18]

Taking the terms 'true' and 'real' as synonymous helps one to understand what Descartes meant by a 'materially false' idea.

[14] HR I, 161–170.
[15] AT V, 356.
[16] Loc. cit.
[17] AT II, 597.
[18] AT III, 545.

This, he says, is an idea which represents so little reality that its object cannot clearly be distinguished from non-being.[19] The examples he appeals to are the ideas of hot and cold. He assumes that one of these must represent a positive quality, and the other a negative quality, i.e., if hot is positive, then cold is merely its negation. However, he says, our ideas of hot and cold are so confused as to offer no grounds for deciding which is the positive quality and which its negation. Neither idea has enough objective reality to qualify for the title of a 'true' idea.

More important is his description of ideas in terms of completeness and adequacy, two terms which are very closely linked, although not identical in either intension or extension. If an idea is adequate, then it is complete, but completeness does not entail adequacy. To have a complete idea of an object is to include within that idea all the defining characteristics of the object in question, or only those characteristics which cannot be denied of it without contradiction.[20] If these are all included, then the object itself is viewed as complete, for it can exist as an independent entity. Incomplete, and hence inadequate, ideas result from abstraction, for we are deceived into thinking that if one property, like that of being figured, can be abstracted from others, like that of being an extended substance, then it can also exist separately.[21] Our ideas in general are sufficiently adequate or comprehensive for us to be aware when one has been rendered incomplete by abstraction, or when an object has sufficient properties to exist independently;[22] but our ideas can never be entirely adequate. Only God possesses truly adequate ideas and is aware that he does.[23] However, if we begin with a complete idea, perhaps of God or a triangle, then we can increase the adequacy of that idea by drawing out more and more of its consequences, although this process cannot be said to increase the original idea.[24] What Descartes had in mind may be illuminated by an analogy with a semantically sound and complete logical system, all of whose axioms and rules are independent. If we remove one of the axioms or rules, the calculus is no longer complete, for at least one valid well-formed formula is not provable.

[19] HR I, 164–5. For a discussion of the difficulties arising from this definition, see A. Kenny, *Descartes* (New York, 1968), pp. 118–121.
[20] AT III, 475.   [21] HR II, 98.
[22] Loc. cit.   [23] HR II, 97.
[24] HR II, 220–221.

However, it is possible to know the axioms and rules, and to know that the system is semantically complete, without being aware of all the theorems. A complete idea is like the set of axioms and rules, but an adequate idea is like a system in which every theorem has been listed.

Descartes' claim that our ideas may grow in adequacy without being increased suggests the distinction which Gewirth made between the direct and the interpretive content of our ideas;[25] or perhaps Descartes' own distinction between the idea "taken materially, as an act of my understanding . . . or . . . taken objectively, as the thing which is represented by this act."[26] In one sense, what we are aware of is static, unchanging, and immediately given to us; but in another sense, it is full of potentiality. It may become more confused or more adequate, depending upon the clarity of our thought. It is a little like a kaleidoscope. The bits of glass are given and do not increase, but the number of different patterns perceived is ever-growing. We do not go outside our idea, we work with it, and as we work we see what was never seen before. The systematic content of our ideas is enlarged, but in the material sense we are not getting new ideas, any more than we acquire a new kaleidoscope for every new pattern. As a result ideas taken objectively must be seen to be independent of the perceiver in a way which ideas taken materially cannot be.

The most significant predicates that can be attached to an idea are 'clear' and 'distinct', for it is only a clear and distinct idea that can be the object of certain knowledge. However, before I begin to examine the meaning of these terms for Descartes, it must be noted that they were often applied to the act rather than the object of perception. Descartes sometimes speaks of clear and distinct ideas or notions or perceptions, but he also frequently speaks of conceiving, perceiving or understanding clearly and distinctly.[27] I will use the adjectival rather than the adverbial form.

[25] Gewirth, A., 'Clearness and Distinctness in Descartes', *Philosophy* 18 (1942), p. 23.
[26] HR I, 138.
[27] A selection of the different phrases he used is as follows: 'une perception claire et distincte' (AT IX, 44); claram & distinctam perceptionem' (AT VII, 61); 'clara & distincta idea' (AT VII 53); 'l'idée claire & distincte' (AT IX, 105); 'les notions claires & distinctes (AT III, 395); 'clarè & distinctè intelligo' (AT VII, 80); 'on conçoit clairement & distinctement' (AT II, 38); 'clarè & distinctè percipio' (AT VII, 68); 'nous appercevons clairement & distinctement' (AT IX, p. 43).

Descartes' only definition of clearness and distinctness comes in the *Principles* and must be quoted in full:

> I term that clear which is present and apparent to an attentive mind, in the same way as we assert that we see objects clearly when, being present to the regarding eye they operate upon it with sufficient strength. But the distinct is that which is so precise and different from other objects that it contains within itself nothing but what is clear.[28]

Given this definition, one could take 'clear' as denoting some kind of immediate awareness about which one cannot be mistaken and draw an analogy between clear perceptions or clear ideas and our sensations, sense data, sensings, or any other favoured locution. Such an interpretation is easily supported, for Descartes speaks of the jaundiced man who sees snow clearly and distinctly as yellow,[29] and he remarks "We have a clear or distinct knowledge of pain, colour, and other things of the sort when we consider them simply as sensations or thoughts."[30] He appeals to the example of severe pain to show how a perception may be clear without being distinct.[31] However, I find the analogy drawn between a clear idea and our sensing of sense data or consciousness of sensations somewhat misleading. The immediate awareness of a sensation seems to be different in nature from the immediate awareness of a concept, for I expect my claim that I am at this moment aware of painful sensations to arouse considerably more interest and agitation than my claim that I am at this moment aware of the concept 'pain'. Moreover, we are presumably not aware of all our sensations with equal clarity, for we can have obscure aches and pains, we can be puzzled about the relative blackness of two lines, we can be uncertain about colours. Nor does the degree of our attentiveness make any difference to these cases. A sharp pain will force itself upon our consciousness, but concentration will not make an obscure ache less obscure. Finally, it must be noted that while Descartes does use the example of sensations on a number of occasions, at other times he claims that sensations are always misleading: "In matters perceived by sense alone, however clearly, certainty does not

[28] HR I, 237.
[29] HR II, 43.
[30] HR I, 248; Cf. HR I 238.
[31] HR I, 237.

exist . . . If, then, any certitude does exist, it remains that it must be found only in the clear perceptions of the intellect."[32] While it is arguable that "the clear perception of the intellect" may in fact have as object some kind of sense datum, it is obvious that Descartes was not primarily interested in these phenomena, and hence that any theory based upon treatment of them is likely to be unreliable.

Whatever is the case with ideas of sense data, I do not think that Descartes wished to assert that the clearness of ideas as concepts consisted simply in one's immediate awareness of them for this would entail both that one had a clear idea of anything upon which one was reflecting, and that any of the empirical concepts, such as 'dog', 'cat', and 'table', which people learn to handle at an early age, could be said to be clear. He seems to have believed that there was a group of ideas such that whenever we reflect upon the contents of our mind, we are immediately aware of these ideas. They include such notions as 'substance', 'extension', 'thought', and 'God . Thus, there must be at least two kinds of clear ideas. There are sensations or sense data which are clear, if at all, only at the moment they are sensed; and there are innate ideas, which are conceptual in nature and can be said to be clear even when they are not actually perceived or reflected upon. How Descartes distinguished between these clear ideas and acquired concepts is difficult to determine, but the distinction is certainly there.

It should be added that innate ideas are presumably immediately apparent to the reflecting mind in the same way as the meaning of a familiar word is immediately understood when one comes across it. Descartes would not wish to say that recognizing the innateness of a particular idea consisted simply in recognizing it as an idea ever-present in the mind; a grasp of the significance of the idea is also implied. We both see and know what we see, although whether what we see has any external referent or not may not be immediately determinable. We have an innate idea of extension, according to Descartes, but we do not know that there are extended objects until we have considered what is entailed by the innate idea of God.

Fresh difficulties are raised at this point by the lack of precision in Descartes' account of innate ideas. Sometimes he

[32] HR II, 42.

suggested that to have an innate idea was simply to have "a disposition or propensity" for acquiring ideas in the presence of the right stimulus;[33] but at another time he wrote that a child in its mother's womb has innate ideas of all self-evident truths no less than adults do when they are not paying attention.[34] "We already possess within us the idea of a true triangle;"[35] just as we possess the idea of God; and although they are not always present "we possess the faculty of summoning up" these ideas.[36] If these ideas are indeed readily available, then all we need is an attentive mind for them to become apparent and hence clear; but if we have only a propensity to acquire them, reflection will have to be preceded by the appropriate experiences or conditions for aware-ness of them to result. Moreover, Descartes seems to couple the dispositional account of innate ideas with the claim that all our ideas are in some sense innate, including those of pain, colour and sound.[37] If this account of innate ideas were adopted, my previous explanation of these ideas would have to be modified, so that clear ideas were identified not with all innate ideas, but only with those that do not need a specific experience to bring them into play. The ideas of pain and red presumably only appear "on the occasion of certain corporeal movements," but ideas like that of God cannot be so limited.

The claim that an innate idea, or a certain kind of innate idea, is clear in so far as it must always be immediately apparent to the reflecting mind is not sufficient to explain all Descartes's uses of the word 'clear'. He remarks, for instance, that if one considers substance and its attributes of existence and duration, one cannot have a clear idea of one attribute without the other.[38] In other words, if I am to say what I mean by 'existence' as predicated of substance, I must employ 'duration' in my definition and vice versa. On the other hand, two clear ideas can be rendered unclear or obscure if I conjoin them, as in the case of the finite and the infinite;[39] but a fictitious idea, synthesized by us, can be analyzed clearly and distinctly.[40] These remarks are reminiscent of the account he has already given of a complete idea as containing all, and presumably only, defining characteristics; and it seems that either the clarity of some ideas is a function of one's under-

[33] HR I, 442–443.
[35] HR II, 228.
[37] HR I, 442–3.
[39] AT V, 161.
[34] AT III, 424.
[36] HR II, 73.
[38] HR I, 245.
[40] HR II, 20.

standing of the concept in question, rather than of one's immediate awareness, or that one can only be said to be immediately aware of a concept if one can give a full definition of the word which expresses that concept. To adopt either alternative as exhausting the meaning Descartes attached to 'clear' would prevent one from referring to a pain sensation as clear, for to argue that the immediate awareness of a pain sensation must either include or be dependent upon understanding of the concept 'pain' is to go beyond the problem of the immediate awareness of sensations to the problem of making judgements about these sensations or categorizing them in some way. It is also to introduce the possibility of making a mistake about whatever it is that one is immediately aware of, which precludes these sensations from being the objects of certain knowledge. Thus we have further support for the division of clear ideas into clear ideas of sensations and clear ideas of concepts.

Descartes is no more consistent in his use of the word 'distinct' than he is in his use of the word 'clear'. For instance, his reference to the jaundiced man 'clearly and distinctly' perceiving the snow as yellow fits in with his definition in so far as the snow is seen as distinct from the people walking about in it, the sky above and so on; but it is inconsistent with his actual use of the word 'distinct' in other passages. Usually, the predicate 'distinct' seems to suggest two things: that the idea in question is complete, and that we have an adequate basis for making some sort of judgment, though only the second applies to ideas of sensations. For instance, my ideas of the earth, sky and stars are not distinct, because the bare ideas give me no basis for judging whether the earth and sky exist, or whether they are like my sensations.[41] Again, a severe pain is perceived clearly but not distinctly because I confuse the perception of the pain with my judgment about its nature, i.e. I tend to think that the pain has a location and a physical cause, although this may not be justifiable.[42] Of course, Descartes does occasionally suggest that if we concentrate very carefully we may have distinct ideas even of pains, for we may manage to forget our notion of a cut finger altogether and focus on the bare sensation so successfully as to justify us in making a judgment about that sensation, though he does not tell us what such a judgment might be.

[41] HR I, 158.   [42] HR I, 237.
H

Some of Descartes' remarks in his discussion of the distinct ideas of concepts seem to suggest that a distinct idea is also a complete idea. For instance, a clear and distinct idea of substance will include the idea of its attributes.[43] But other remarks suggest that it is clearness rather than distinctness that entails completeness for he claims that we can have a distinct understanding of duration, order and number if we do not mingle with these ideas what belongs to the conception of substance.[44] Presumably a complete idea, since it is of a complete object, would have to include the defining characteristics of substance. This raises a further question about the presence of good grounds for judgment. Only if we have a distinct as well as a clear idea of a sensation can we make valid judgments; but if a clear idea of a concept is a complete idea we already have good grounds for making judgments; whereas if a distinct idea can be incomplete, we will not have sufficient grounds.

To give a plausible interpretation of the terms 'clear' and 'distinct' which at the same time covers all Descartes' uses of these terms is rendered almost impossible by the way in which Descartes used the word 'idea' and by his general imprecision. On the one hand, one must make a distinction between what is said about sensations and what is said about concepts, but on the other hand, one must refrain from trying to make a sharp distinction between the properties of a clear idea and the properties of a distinct idea. With these caveats in mind, a few concluding statements can be made. The idea of a pain sensation is clear and distinct only if it is immediately apparent, and only if the mind refrains from making false judgments on the basis of the sensation in question. The case of the idea of a concept, or the idea as a concept, is more complex and more important. A clear and distinct idea in this sense must be both apparent to any reflecting mind and understood by any reflecting mind. It contains all and only what is essential for this understanding, and hence, it contains grounds for the making of judgments about the idea. These characteristics do not belong only to concepts, but also to propositions. 'I think, therefore I exist' for instance, is a truth both immediately perceived and immediately understood when one sets out to examine the contents of the mind; in contrast

[43] HR I, 245.
[44] HR I, 241.

with the proposition 'I think, therefore I exist and have blue eyes,' it contains nothing extraneous; and it contains all the grounds we need for making the judgment that it is a true proposition, i.e., we do not need to appeal for extra information or to carry out empirical tests, any more than we do when we say '2+3=5' or 'I am now in pain.' Equally, we have here a firm foundation for making further judgments about what the *cogito* entails.

The only other remarks of note which Descartes has to make about clear and distinct ideas, is that they may exhibit varying degrees of clearness and distinctness. For instance, the idea of God 'may become the most true, most clear and most distinct of all the ideas which are in my mind.'[45] Presumably an idea becomes more clear and distinct as it becomes more adequate, and the degree of adequacy to which it can attain depends both upon our intellectual endeavour and upon the degree of reality or richness of being contained in the object of our idea. There are more truths to be discovered about God than about a triangle.

We must now consider the question of whether clearness and distinctness is a satisfactory criterion. The most immediately obvious objection is that it is perfectly possible to have a seemingly clear and distinct idea of what is false;[46] and although Descartes was often called upon to deal with this point, he did so less by rational argument than by a declaration of faith in his own doctrines. He felt that if an idea does not provide good evidence, if it does not in fact justify a claim to knowledge, then it cannot be clear and distinct, although it may at first sight *seem* so. We cannot ultimately be deceived about the having of a clear and distinct idea if we examine our ideas with honest care; but Descartes claimed that we could be prevented from carrying out such an examination by the unreasoned prejudices we have been absorbing from our youth onwards.[47] How else could he explain the fact that not all men admitted to having a clear and distinct idea of God, whilst others claimed to have clear and distinct ideas of false gods? Descartes avoided the pitfall of introducing yet further criteria which would distinguish clear and distinct ideas from those seemingly so; but he only did so by saying in

[45] HR I, 166.
[46] HR I, 220.
[47] HR II, 226; Cf. HR II, 42.

effect that we can only be deceived when we have not looked hard enough, and that we have only looked hard enough when we cease to be deceived. The legitimacy of such a move is, at best, highly dubious. Moreover, Kenny suggests that Descartes did fall into the trap of rejecting seemingly clear and distinct ideas on the grounds that they are not true, when the only criterion we have for truth is clearness and distinctness![48]

The strongest point he put forward in support of clear and distinct ideas was that they were indubitable. However, one may mean various things by 'p is indubitable', and it is necessary to canvass several interpretations before Descartes' claim can be evaluated. Firstly, one may mean that it is logically impossible to doubt p, provided that one understands what p means and is uttering it as a statement and not simply as an exercise in voice production or part of a play. I am using 'logically impossible' in a wide sense, to include not only those statements whose negation involves a logical contradiction, but some which are dependent upon the context of their utterance, like first person reports of experience and self-verifying statements like 'I exist.' The denial of the last two types of statement is not a contradiction, but there is something more than psychological absurdity attached to such denials and doubts expressed by the speaker, however one may wish to describe it.

Descartes would have accepted the logical impossibility of doubting that he existed, or that he was in severe pain, but he did not accept a class of truths whose denial is a logical contradiction in the full sense. It is true that he writes in one of his letters that what is 'repugnant to our ideas is absolutely impossible and implies a contradiction'[49] and to illustrate this he cites the impossibility of an indivisible extended atom; but this kind of contradiction is contingent, for it rests upon God and the immutability of his laws. Descartes places a very great emphasis on the power of God, and where most scholastic philosophers had been content to refer to the 'eternal truths', such as the truths of mathematics, as being ideas in the mind of God, Descartes insisted that they were truths not only known by God, but created by him.[50] As a product of his intellect they were also, and more importantly, a

[48]A. Kenny, op. cit., 198–9.
[49]AT III, 476.
[50]AT I, 152–3. Cf. AT I, 145–6; AT II, 138; AT IV, 118–9.

product of his will, which entailed, for Descartes, that they could have been otherwise. God could even have brought it about that the radii of a circle were not equal. [51] Descartes agrees that we cannot comprehend this fact, but this argues a limitation of our understanding rather than of God's power. We know that these eternal truths as established, and as known by us, are immutable; but this is a consequence of our knowledge of God's immutability and of his desire not to mislead us. Hence the fact that we can treat some truths as if they were strictly analytic is contingent upon God's nature, and it follows that we cannot use a logical criterion to pick out the paradigm case of certain truth that Descartes was searching for. The criterion had to be some non-logical property of such ideas or statements.

Even if one were to agree that some of the ideas Descartes called clear and distinct were indubitable in the first sense, it does not follow that they are indubitable because they are clear and distinct; nor does it follow that all of Descartes' clear and distinct ideas are indubitable in this way, especially when analyticity has been discarded. Hence, one may turn to a second sense of 'p is indubitable,' namely, 'it is psychologically impossible to doubt that p.' Here we are on much stronger ground with respect to Descartes' expressed beliefs, for he does indeed seem to accept the notion of psychological impossibility. It is not possible for me to withhold assent from what is clearly understood, he writes.[52] We cannot refrain from accepting our clear and distinct ideas as true, or bring ourselves to deny any mathematical truths.[53] In so far as a clear idea is one of which we are immediately aware, it is true that we cannot doubt that we have this particular idea; but, except where sense datum statements or the immediate report of sensations are concerned, having a clear and distinct idea involves more than immediate awareness, and what we are said not to be able to doubt is not the having of the idea but the content of the idea. Hence the appeal to psychological impossibility is not satisfactory, for it is always possible to doubt even a logical truth.

A further difficulty is raised here by what he says of the atheist, who has clear and distinct ideas but can never be entirely free from doubt since he has no faith in God to rescue him from

[51] AT I, 152.
[52] AT III, 64. Cf. HR II, 42.
[53] HR I, 158-9.

the pitfalls of scepticism.[54] If a belief in God is necessary, then clearness and distinctness can never by itself be enough to ensure than an idea is indubitable. Moreover, even were it psychologically impossible for any man to doubt an idea, no matter what his beliefs, this would only tell us something about man's psychology, not about the idea.

Can one, then, claim that a clear and distinct idea is indubitable in the third sense, whereby 'p is indubitable' means 'p ought not to be doubted'? To make this latter claim is to commit oneself to the assertions that p contains within itself no grounds for doubt, and, moreover, that one has adequate evidence for p. What will be accepted as adequate evidence varies in accordance with the type of statement being considered, and the class of statements that ought not to be doubted will include all those which it is logically impossible to doubt, as well as many ordinary empirical statements, but it may exclude some of those statements which a given individual finds it psychologically impossible to doubt. So far as Descartes was concerned, the notion of adequate evidence collapses into the notion of containing no grounds for doubt. His search for an internal criterion precluded any other possibility. Given this limitation, he does indeed seem to think that clear and distinct ideas are indubitable in the sense that they offer no grounds for doubt. In a letter to Regius he contrasts knowledge (*scientia*) with opinion (*persuasio*), saying that in the case of opinion there is always something which may impel us to doubt, whereas knowledge must be supported by such strong reasons that no stronger can ever be found to attack it.[55] Since the having of a clear and distinct idea is generally regarded by Descartes as a sufficient condition for a claim to know, it would seem that the idea must be self-supporting. The 'strong' reasons must be intrinsic to the idea. That this is the case is suggested by Descartes' uses of the words 'clear' and 'distinct' to refer to a complete idea which contains within itself all the necessary grounds for making a sound judgment about that idea. Any grounds for attacking a judgment about that idea must then be external to it, and hence will not be strong enough to justify doubt.

But once more Descartes' arguments are vitiated by what he has to say of the atheist. It seems that one must disregard either

[54] HR II, 39.
[55] AT III, 65.

the claim that the clear and distinct idea is complete or the claim that an atheist does not have sufficient grounds for being sure of the judgments he makes. Either course will destroy theories which were dear to Descartes, and either course will preclude true indubitability.

But even if these internal difficulties are disregarded, there remains an objection which must be fatal. Why is it that we ought not to doubt a clear and distinct idea; and how is it that their possession, itself open to question, can justify our claims to know about such matters as the existence of God and the nature of substance? If Descartes appeals simply to the intrinsic nature of the idea, then he can be told that the examination of an idea will tell us only about that idea and nothing further. If he appeals to God as the guarantor of the truth of clear and distinct ideas, then the attack can be turned to his proof of God's existence and the circularity of his arguments. If he puts it forward as a matter of faith, then he could be accused of denying his attempt to counter skepticism by rational argument. Finally, if he justifies it on the grounds that an idea is only clear and distinct if it justifies a claim to know, then he can be accused of offering not a test of clearness and distinctness, but an analytic proposition of no particular value.

Although Descartes struggled to defend his criterion, his struggles ended in an impasse. He had made the mistake of trying to prove too much. He had wanted to develop an introspective technique by which he could be sure of recognizing those ideas which were objects of certain knowledge; but such an enterprize was doomed from the start. He could only escape from the objection that nothing about an idea can justify us in making judgment about its external reference by entering into an uneasy and unjustifiable alliance with God; and by such an alliance he negated his claim that a single criterion for true and knowable ideas could be found.

VI

THE PROBLEM OF METAPHYSICAL DOUBT AND ITS REMOVAL[1]

Robert E. Alexander

Those (like Arnauld in the Fourth Objection) who wish to impute 'circular reasoning' to Descartes' epistemology, usually see this issue arising in the Third Meditation. One way of describing this circle is that 'in the order of reasons' Descartes proves his own existence and later proves the existence of a non-deceptive God. However, since there is no certain knowledge of anything without already having proved God's existence, these proofs presuppose the conclusion of the second. I believe an equivalent way of formulating this is by saying that there is a general rule or test of truth against which a metaphysical doubt is raised. The circle comes about since the only way the doubt can be removed is by using the rule itself to prove that God is non-deceptive.

If we use 'absolute' to refer to what is true or false for God, we have the following possible results of using the rule.

R1—'The rule yields *relative* truth only, not absolute truth.'
R2—'The rule yields *absolute* truth, since God guarantees its application to all propositions.'
R3—'The rule yields *absolute* truth with no guarantee needed.

The issues raised by the doubt and the circle depend on the rule of truth, so the first section will deal with it. This will include developing the theses that the rule of truth (clarity and distinctness) yields necessary truth and that it yields absolute truth (i.e., Descartes does not hold the relativity position, R1). The second section will develop the charge of circularity by showing that the metaphysical doubt is not counterfactual and that it applies to intuitions, not only conclusions of deductions. I will argue in the third section that there need be no circle of any sort, since Des-

[1] I wish to gratefully acknowledge the support of the Canada Council and the helpful criticisms of Professor William Abbott.

cartes ought to hold only R3. This will conclude with a discussion of the oddity of the metaphysical doubt.

I

Descartes wants to 'establish [a] firm and permanent structure in the sciences.'[2] To do this he puts forward his famous method of doubt by supposing that 'some evil genius not less powerful than deceitful, has employed his whole energies in deceiving me.'[3] He intends to accept as true only what can withstand such a doubt. In the Second Meditation he finds his 'Archimedian point'—the *cogito ergo sum*.

> I am, I exist, is necessarily true each time that I pronounce it, or that I mentally conceive it, [since even if the evil genius] deceive[s] me as much as he will, he can never cause me to be nothing, so long as I think that I am something.[4]

Thinking (whether it is deceptive or not) is a mental activity which necessarily presupposes an actor or agent. Because of what is involved in the *cogito*, we can say that Descartes knows two things for certain at this stage: 'I am' and 'I am a thing which thinks'.[5]

Descartes is interested in the *cogito* not only as a piece of factual knowledge, but also and more significantly as something from which he can derive principles which will make up the foundation for science. Thus, his immediate concern is to generate a rule or test of truth from his first known truth.

A. *The relation between clarity, distinctness, and necessary truth.* I will now try to clarify what Descartes thinks is involved in the rule. It is introduced in the Third Meditation two paragraphs before he mentions the slight, metaphysical doubt.

> Certainly in this first knowledge [that I am a thing which thinks] there is nothing that assures me of its truth, excepting the clear and distinct perception of that which I state, which would not indeed suffice to assure me that what I say is true, if it could ever happen that a thing which I conceived so clearly and distinctly could be false, and accordingly it seems to me

[2] HR I, 144.
[3] HR I, 148.
[4] HR I, 150.
[5] We learn that this is not the first knowledge *simpliciter*, but only the first knowledge of anything that exists. See Principle X.

that already I can establish as a general rule that all things which I perceive very clearly and very distinctly are true.[6]

In this passage Descartes derives a rule of evidence and truth from the *cogito*. We are all familiar with his result which is founded on clarity and distinctness. But how are we to understand the qualification that clarity and distinctness is insufficient to guarantee truth 'if it could ever happen that a thing which I conceived so clearly and distinctly could be false?'

L. J. Beck, in commenting on this passage in *The Metaphysics of Descartes*, holds that

the criterion itself is subjected by Descartes to a condition: that is, that a proposition is clearly and distinctly perceived to be true only when every possibility of its being false is excluded.[7]

This is a plausible interpretation of this slippery passage, and one with which I agree. However, it can also be considered as a preview of the metaphysical doubt which follows almost immediately. From this point of view, the qualification shows Descartes' concern about justifying the rule. Beck's interpretation is more important for us at this stage, so I will take up the issue of whether this qualifier does restrict the application of the rule.

Descartes has just claimed that clarity and distinctness is the only thing that assures him of the truth of the *cogito*. Then, in the context of the metaphysical doubt, he says that the *cogito* is based on the fact that its opposite is a 'manifest contradiction.'

Let who will deceive me, He can never cause me to be nothing while I think that I am, or some day cause it to be true to say that I have never been, it now being true to say that I am, or that two and three make more or less than five, or any such thing in which I see a manifest contradiction.[8]

The fact that he does not refer to clarity and distinctness here (even though he has just said that 'there is nothing that assures me of its [the *cogito*] truth, excepting the clear and distinct perception of that which I state') seems to mean that Descartes does not intend to draw any distinction between clarity and

[6] HR I, 158.
[7] L. J. Beck, *The Metaphysics of Descartes: A Study of the Meditations*, (Oxford, 1965), p. 142.
[8] HR I, 158–9.

distinctness and denial of a contradiction; otherwise he would be giving up the rule, but there is no indication of that. And we have seen that Descartes referred to the *cogito* as 'necessarily true' in the Second Meditation. In the Synopsis he says that 'mind . . . recognizes that it is however absolutely impossible that it does not itself exist.'[9] This impossibility is called a 'contradiction' in Principle VII[10]. So, a proposition which is clear and distinct is a proposition whose opposite is a contradiction.

If my argument is correct, it has the following important consequence. A proposition which is really clear and distinct is also the opposite of a contradiction, and this means that it is an analytic or necessarily true proposition. In short, the correct application of the rule yields necessary truths. I will not propose an analysis of the concept of necessary truth, but it is clear that Descartes construes necessity in such a way that 'I, while I think, exist' is so as well as the more usual examples of 'two and three are five' and 'what is done cannot be undone.'[11]

B. *R1 is not Descartes' position as Frankfurt maintains.* What kind of truth does the rule yield? Though I will not discuss Descartes' theory of truth in a general way, we have seen that it at least yields necessary truth. Could such truth nevertheless be absolutely false from God's point of view, i.e., could R1 be his position?

Harry G. Frankfurt maintains that it is when he says that

the *Meditations* is designed not so much to prove that what is intuited is true as to show that there are no reasonable grounds for doubting this. Now it may be objected that in that case he leaves the main question still open, since it may be that what we intuit is sometimes false even if we can have no reasonable grounds for supposing so. Whatever may be the weight of this objection, it bears against Descartes' doctrines, and not my interpretation of them. Indeed, some confirmation for my interpretation is to be seen in the fact that Descartes acknowledges that an objection of this sort may be raised against his position.[12]

[9] HR I, 140.   [10] HR I, 221.

[11] For a discussion of the kind of necessity involved in the *cogito*, see Jaakko Hintikka, '*Cogito, Ergo Sum*: Inference or Performance', *Philosophical Review*, LXXI, (1962) and Harry G. Frankfurt, 'Descartes' Discussion of His Existence in the Second Meditation', *Philosophical Review*, LXXV, (1966).

[12] Harry G. Frankfurt, 'Descartes' Validation of Reason', *American Philosophical Quarterly*, II, (1965), p. 156.

This objection is raised as a difficulty in the fourth section of the Second Reply. Descartes is here redeveloping the argument for certainty which culminates in such truths as the *cogito*. He says that we can use the rule to determine the truth, if we think we have 'rightly perceived' a given proposition.

> Further, if this conviction [of the truth] is so strong that we have no reason to doubt concerning that of the truth of which we have persuaded ourselves, there is nothing more to inquire about; we have here all the certainty that can reasonably be desired. What is it to us, though perchance some one feigns that, of the truth of which we are so firmly persuaded, appears false to God or to an Angel, and hence is, absolutely speaking, false? What heed do we pay to that absolute falsity, when we by no means believe that it exists or even suspect its existence? We have assumed a conviction so strong that nothing can remove it, and this persuasion is clearly the same as perfect certitude.[13]

From this passage Frankfurt comes to the conclusion that 'the notions of absolute truth and absolute falsity are irrelevant to the purposes of inquiry.'[14] And so, his position is what I have called R1, viz., that the rule yields relative truth only, not absolute truth.

There are two quite different reasons for treating absolute falsity as irrelevant. Frankfurt's reason is that absolute falsity is irrelevant because absolute truth is irrelevant, too. Descartes' reason, as Anthony Kenny points out,[15] is that absolute falsity is irrelevant because clear and distinct propositions are absolutely true. Such falsity is of no concern to Descartes because it can be dealt with in terms of clarity and distinctness.

This is shown just five paragraphs later where Descartes again considers the 'objection' that the rule might yield absolute falsity.

> Again there is no difficulty though some one feign that the truth appear false to God or to an Angel, because the evidence of our perception does not allow us to pay any attention to such a fiction.[16]

---

[13] HR II, 41.   [14] Loc. cit.

[15] Anthony Kenny, *Descartes: A Study of His Philosophy*, (New York, 1968), p. 195.

[16] HR II, 42.

Contrary to what Frankfurt believes, Descartes does *not* 'acknowledge that an objection of this sort may be raised against his position.' The objection is 'feigned'; the possibility that the rule might yield absolute falsity is a 'fiction'. After all, if the rule were unable to cope with absolute falsity, then Descartes would end up being deceived.

At this point one might object that the concept of absolute falsity is empty or, as some prefer to say, is meaningless, since deception which cannot in principle be detected is not deception at all. I have some sympathy with this thesis, but Descartes does not. He is not disturbed by the concept of absolute falsity in what was quoted above nor in Principle V where he talks of being 'always' and 'continually' deceived.[17] He is only worried about whether his mind is such that it exemplifies such a concept. Thus, the objection fails, not for the reason that Frankfurt thought (viz., relative truth or falsity is the best man can obtain), but because Descartes believes he can obtain absolute truth. Instead of Frankfurt's gaining 'some confirmation of my [his] interpretation' from this passage, I believe there is a disconfirmation only five paragraphs later.

II

The charge of circularity develops as a result of Descartes' introduction of the slight, metaphysical doubt immediately after he states the general rule of truth. Things 'very simple and easy in the sphere of arithmetic or geometry . . . e.g. that two and three together made five,'[18] seem to be indubitable. Yet

> Certainly if I judged that since such matters could be doubted, this would not have been so for any other reason than that it came into my mind that perhaps a God might have endowed me with such a nature that I may have been deceived even concerning things which seemed to me most manifest. . . . it is easy to Him, if He wishes it, to cause me to err, even in matters in which I believe my self to have the best evidence. And, on the other hand, always when I direct my attention to things which I believe my self to perceive very clearly, I am so persuaded of their truth that I let myself break out into words such as these: Let who will deceive me, He can never cause

[17] HR I, 220.
[18] HR I, 158.

me to be nothing while I think that I am, or some day cause it to be true to say that . . . two and three make more or less than five, or any such thing in which I see a manifest contradiction. And, certainly, since I have no reason to believe that there is a God who is a deceiver, and as I have not yet satisfied my self that there is a God at all, the reason for doubt which depends on this opinion alone is very slight, and so to speak metaphysical. But in order to be able altogether to remove it, I must inquire whether there is a God as soon as the occasion presents itself; and if I find that there is a God, I must also inquire whether He may be a deceiver; for without a knowledge of these two truths [viz., the existence of a non-deceptive God] I do not see that I can ever be certain of anything.[19]

At this stage in 'the order of reasons,' i.e., the chronological order of Descartes' arguments, he has not yet established God's existence. However, since there is no certain knowledge of anything without already having a proof of a non-deceptive God, the certainty of this proof presupposes its own conclusion.

We can also consider the same problem in terms of the rule or test of truth. In the above reference, Descartes' thoughts about being deceived even by the most obvious clearly refers to the rule, since the most obvious is clear and distinct perception (mentioned in the rule).[20] Thus, his doubts are doubts about whether the rule will do the job, whether even the most obvious is good enough to yield the truth. His conclusion is that apparently the best is not good enough, since the best only yields truth if we have a proof for God's existence. But the only rule available for the latter is an (as yet) unjustified rule, so to have both a justified rule and a proof of God's existence entails the circle. This is Arnauld's formulation of 'circular reasoning' in the Forth Reply.

But we can be sure that God exists, only because we clearly and evidently perceive that; therefore prior to being certain that God exists, we should be certain that whatever we clearly and evidently perceive is true.[21]

The main issues that arise from the remarkable passage on

[19] HR I, 158–9.
[20] See also the Fifth Meditation (*Ibid.*, I, 183–4) where clarity and distinctness is explicitly referred to as the object of the doubt only God can remove.
[21] HR II, 92.

metaphysical doubt are the following: whether the doubt is counterfactual; what the doubt applies to; and how we are to understand Descartes' apparent ability and also inability to doubt that 'two and three are five'.

A. *The metaphysical doubt is not counterfactual.* The doubt refers to the possibility that we have such a deceptive nature that even the best evidence is not good enough. Can I doubt 'two and three are five?' This doubt is introduced by the hypothetical 'if'. A few lines below Descartes admits that the opposite of this arithmetic proposition is a manifest contradiction and, therefore, is itself indubitable. It appears, then, that the antecedent ('If I judged that such matters could be doubted') is false. For this reason the doubt appears to be so slight as to never get off the ground.

This is an inadequate solution on two counts. First, instead of concluding that his nature is such that it cannot be deceived about what is most obvious in at least some cases (e.g., the *cogito* and 'two and three are five'), Descartes claims that the doubt must be removed by a proof of a non-deceptive God. Since he does not have this proof yet, and he must still allow a deceptive nature, the Cartesian circle again rears its ugly head.

Second, in Principle V, the doubt is not hypothetical at all, but categorical.

> We *shall* also doubt of all other things [i.e., non-sensible things] which have formerly seemed to us quite certain, even of the demonstrations of mathematics and of its principles which we formerly thought quite self-evident. [One of the reasons is that] He may . . . have desired to create us in such a way that we *shall* always be deceived, even in the things that we believe ourselves to know best. . . .[22]

This occurs before the *cogito* and God's existence and is only removed in Principle XXX after it is shown that God is no deceiver. In removing this doubt Descartes identifies a non-deceptive nature with an affirmation that the rule of clarity and distinctness never fails to yield the truth. Such a justification

> should deliver us from the supreme doubt which encompassed us when we did not know whether our nature had been such that

[22] HR I, 220.

we had been deceived in things that seemed most clear . . . .
The truths of mathematics should now be above suspicion,
for they are of the clearest.[23]

Thus, the doubt is reaffirmed as applying even to two and three are
five in the absence of a proof of the existence of God and is now
described as 'supreme,' rather than 'slight.' Whatever description
we use, we can conclude about the doubt both: that its import is
serious because the rule must be immune to it; and that it is
categorical, not counterfactual.

    B. *The doubt is intended to apply to conclusions only.* When
Descartes says that he can never be certain of anything without
knowing that a non-deceptive God exists, does he include in
'anything' the *cogito*, two and three are five, and the proof of God?
If so, we again have the circle. Since this seems too obvious for
him to have fallen into, we will look further before coming to a
decision.

    Principle XIII, titled '*In what sense the knowledge of all other
things depends on the knowledge of God,*' picks out deductions
whose premises are no longer attended to. These conclusions
(like 'the three angles of a triangle are equal to two right angles')
are subject to the metaphysical doubt until the mind is 'acquainted
with its creator'.[24] However, the next Principle refers to the fact
that God's existence can be '*demonstrated*'. This would leave him
in the bind of guaranteeing deductions by a deduction, such that
the conclusion that God exists (if the premises were no longer
attended to) would depend on itself.

    He does seem to leave himself open to this objection in his
answer to Anauld's charge of circularity.

For first, we are sure that God exists because we have attended
to the proofs that established this fact; but afterwards it is
enough for us to remember that we have perceived something
clearly, in order to be sure that it is true: but this would not
suffice, unless we knew that God existed and that he did not
deceive us.[25]

The Second Reply gives the clearest statement of Descartes'
intent.

[23] HR I, 231.
[24] HR I, 224.
[25] HR II, 115.

Thirdly, when I said that *we could know nothing with certainty unless we were first aware that God existed,* I announced in express terms that I referred only to the science apprehending such conclusions *as can recur in memory without attending further to the proofs which led me to make them.* Further, knowledge of first principles is not usually called science by dialecticians.[26]

The *cogito* is expressly excluded from the doubt, because it

is a primitive act of knowledge derived from no syllogistic reasoning. He who says, '*I think, hence I am, or exist,*' does not deduce existence from thought by a syllogism, but [recognizes it] by a simple act of mental vision . . . .[27]

But God's existence is not explicitly excluded from the doubt. However, it may be that Descartes would want to argue that one sees that God's essence necessarily includes his existence by a simple act of mental vision too, even though he often refers to it as a demonstration or proof.

In any case, whether God's existence is an intuition or a deduction, we still have the apparent inconsistency (established in II. A) of doubting and yet being unable to doubt two and three are five. Given that it is listed with the *cogito* as something whose opposite is a manifest contradiction, it is plausible to assume that it is no mere conclusion of a deduction, but is rather an intuition. Whenever Descartes wants to give an example of a demonstrated conclusion, he uses the geometrical example where 'the three angles are equal to two right angles,' not the arithmetical one.[28] Since this is the case, and since Principle V includes the metaphysical doubt of first principles of mathematics as well as demonstrations, Descartes' intended restrictions to conclusions is not compatible with what he says here or in the Third Meditation.

Prima facie, we ought to take what Descartes says in the *Replies* as more authoritative than the *Meditations,* since the former is his considered attempt to clarify and defend the latter. But in this case the third section of the Second Reply does not seem to clarify the Third Meditation, because they are about different things. In the latter he is concerned with a distinction between

[26] HR II, 38.
[27] *Ibid.*
[28] HR I, 184. See also HR II, p. 39 and HR I, 224.

I

directly and indirectly doubting something and the sort of things referred to are intuitions, not only conclusions. In the next section we will see that there is a way of explicating what Descartes seems to be concerned with in the Third Meditation. And we will see that this analysis might lead him to talk about only doubting conclusions, but that nevertheless he should have talked about a special manner of doubting anything—intuitions included.

III

The key to disentangling God's justificatory role from the alleged circle, according to Kenny, is a distinction between first- and second-order doubt.

> Take the proposition 'What's done cannot be undone.' If I explicitly think of this proposition, Descartes says, I cannot at that moment doubt it, that is, I cannot help judging that it is true. However, though I cannot doubt this proposition while my mind's eye is on it, I can, as it were, turn away from it and doubt it in a roundabout manner. I can refer to it under some general heading, such as 'what seems to me most obvious'; and I can raise the whole question whether everything that seems to me most obvious may not in fact be false . . . . The [metaphysical] axioms are thus generically doubtful while severally indubitable. While in doubt about the author of my nature, I do not know whether the light of nature is a true light or a false light. This second-order doubt is the metaphysical doubt that cannot be removed except by proving the existence of a veracious God.[29]
>
> To engage in metaphysical doubt is . . . to betray the weakness of the human intellect that is incapable of holding intuitions steady [which will] be remedied by the consideration of God's veracity . . . . The simple intuition by itself provides both psychologically and logically the best grounds for accepting its truth. Thus, there is no circle. Deduction is called in question, and deduction is vindicated by intuition. The truth of particular intuitions is never called in question, only the universal trustworthiness of intuition, and in vindicating this universal trustworthiness only individual intuitions are utilized.[30]

This is a very persuasive reconstruction of Descartes' belief that

---

[29] Op. cit., 183-4.   [30] Ibid., 194.

there is a metaphysical doubt which God must remove and that this removal does not involve him in a circle. Because of the importance of the issues involved (some of which have not been made explicit, and some of which I want to disagree with), Kenny's discussion is worth a careful scrutiny.

A. *The metaphysical doubt applies to propositions 'in general' only.* To say that propositions are 'generally doubtful while severally indubitable' is, I assume, the same as to say that 'one can doubt all such propositions, in general, but not in particular.' To be true to the style of the *Meditations*, I will focus on the following open sentence: 'I, Descartes, doubt, in general, all propositions of a certain type.' (The type in question will be specified by one of the three descriptions, D1, etc., discussed below.) The first thing to notice about this sentence is that the phrase 'in general' does not mean something like the phrase 'in most cases, but not in all' as it does in the sentence, 'In general, philosophers have their heads in the clouds.' Descartes does not usually, or customarily, doubt propositions of a certain type; nor does he doubt them serially, one by one, for this would be what is meant by the phrase 'in particular.' Rather, he doubts them *qua* a certain type or under a 'general heading' or description without attending to the content of any instance.

The second thing to notice is that doubting, like believing, is 'referentially opaque', to use Quine's phrase.[31] As I use this expression, a sentence is referentially opaque if and only if it violates Leibniz's Law, i.e., the substitution of co-extensive phrases does not invariably yield the same truth-values. One of Quine's examples is of Tom who believes something about Cicero that he does not believe about Tully because he is unaware that Cicero is Tully.

The referential opacity of doubting is essential for Kenny's argument. If doubting were referentially transparent, then there would be no difference between doubting 'in general' and doubting 'in particular', and thus, there would be no way of turning 'my mind's eye' away from a proposition and 'doubt[ing] it in a roundabout manner.' However, this opacity is not that between two names for the same object as in the standard Tully-Cicero case that Quine was concerned with: that Cicero was also Tully is a contingent matter. Rather, it is the opacity between a propo-

[31] W. V. O. Quine, *Word and Object*, (New York, 1960), ch. IV.

sition with regard to its type only and with regard to it as a particular: this relationship is not contingent.

B. *Descartes ought not appeal to God's veracity to remove the doubt.* It is now time to consider various closures for our open sentence. Consider the following descriptions: D1– 'which are written on this piece of paper;' D2– 'which are most obvious to me;' D3– 'which are clearly and distinctly perceived, i.e., which I cannot doubt.' If we fill in our sentence with D1, so that it reads 'I doubt, in general, all the propositions written on this piece of paper,' no difficulty arises. The propositions are surely doubtful until more is known about them than the mere fact that they are written here, and there is no guarantee (or even liklihood) that they will be indubitable when taken singly. This is not the metaphysical doubt at issue, so D1 is not a plausible candidate for Kenny's 'general heading'.

D3 does not seem to fulfill Kenny's requirements, either. I have shown in section I.A that propositions which are clearly and distinctly perceived (i.e., necessary truths whose opposites are manifest contradictions) are the same as those propositions which cannot be doubted. Thus, our open sentence becomes 'I doubt, in general, all the propositions I cannot doubt.' But this is absurd. Even the phrase 'in general' does not save this from being a manifest contradiction itself.

This leaves us with D2, Kenny's own suggestion. (Descartes' own phrases are 'most manifest' and 'best evidence;' for my purpose I will consider these synonymous with 'most obvious'.)[32] This is the heading most likely to fit his proposal, since it is possible to doubt even what is 'most obvious to me'. However, this doubt is possible *only* in case one is not thinking of any particular kind of obviousness, but is instead just contemplating the possibility that the best kind of obviousness (whatever it might amount to) may not be enough to remove all doubt. This is not a doubt all things considered; rather, it is a prima facie doubt which may or may not stand up under an analysis of what counts as really obvious. This seems to leave room to doubt in

[32] It is not strictly true that 'obvious' is synonymous with 'clear and distinct'. What is obvious is clear and distinct, but not everything that is clear and distinct is obvious. 'Obvious' applies to intuitions, or axioms, only; whereas 'clear and distinct' applies equally to intuitions and deductive conclusions which are themselves not obvious. However, this does not affect my argument, since I am only arguing from what is obvious to what is clear and distinct. See Kenny, *op. cit.*, p. 175.

general what, when confronted in particular, is indubitable. Kenny is implying that Descartes finds himself in a situation similar to the half-hearted Nazi who believes that he hates Jews in general, but has never met a Jew he didn't like!

So, Kenny's argument works when D2 is used, but only *prior* to an analysis of what really counts as being obvious. But at this stage in the order of reasons in the *Meditations* (i.e., where the metaphysical doubt enters in the Third Meditation) this analysis has already taken place. Thus, D2 without such an analysis is not available and yet it should be to make sense of the metaphysical doubt. And Descartes knows (or ought to know from what he says) that D2 with an analysis is equivalent to D3. And since D3 fails to leave room for the doubt, so does D2.

To put this in a slightly different form, Kenny would be correct in maintaining, as it seems he has to, that: (a) doubting is referentially opaque; (b) referential opacity and the phrase 'in general' provide a distinction between doubting propositions *en masse* with respect to certain features only, and doubting them in particular; (c) the above distinction warrants the conclusion that Descartes may doubt all propositions which are most obvious without thereby doubting, e.g., that 'I, Descartes, while I think, exist'— at least, prior to an analysis of what obviousness amounts to. This means that we now have an explanation of the sense in which Descartes holds both R2 and R3. R2 becomes

R2'—'The rule yields absolute truth, since God guarantees its application to propositions *in general*.'

R3 becomes

R3'—'The rule yields absolute truth with no guarantee needed, when applied to propositions *in particular*.'

Thus, Descartes' references to justifying the rule, which occur throughout the *Meditations*, *Replies*, and *Principles*, must be taken in the sense of R2'.

My disagreement with Kenny can be summed up in the following argument:

(i) 'I, Descartes, doubt, in general, all propositions which are most obvious.'

(ii) 'I, Descartes, know that all propositions which are most obvious are propositions which are clear and distinct, i.e., those which I cannot doubt.'

(iii) 'I, Descartes, doubt, in general, all propositions which are
clear and distinct, i.e., those which I cannot doubt.'

Here, Kenny would also be correct in maintaining that (iii) does
not follow from (i) alone. But I have argued that (ii) is available,
and now claim that (i) and (ii) do entail (iii), since knowing that
the terms in (i) and (iii) are co-extensive makes the argument go
through. That is, the second premise renders the reference of (i)
and (iii) transparent with respect to each other and collapses D2
into D3.[33] But (iii) is a contradiction itself because it amounts to
'I doubt what I cannot doubt.' So, R2' becomes untenable and
we are left with R3″ (=R3), viz., *no guarantee of the rule is needed
when applied to propositions in particular nor in general.*

I agree with Kenny that Descartes believes that there is a
metaphysical doubt of propositions when applied in general which
God must remove. I agree that 'the truth of particular intuitions
is never called in question.' I assume that when Kenny says 'only
the universal trustworthiness of intuition' is called in question,
that he means that the rule when applied only in general is called
in question. And I agree with Kenny that 'in vindicating this
universal trustworthiness [of the rule] only individual intuitions
are utilized.'

But there are two alternative ways of using individual intuitions
to vindicate the rule in this way: (a) an intuition *qua* the information
yielded by this token only; (b) an intuition *qua* the information
yielded by any token at all. I agree with Kenny that Descartes
uses the former method, since no other intuition can give us the
necessary information about God as our non-deceptive creator.
However, this is redundant as Descartes has already decided that
the denials of clear and distinct propositions are contradictions.
I have maintained that Descartes has already removed the doubt
about the rule by reference to the *cogito*. The *cogito* does not
vindicate anything in so far as it is merely a piece of information
about my existence. But in so far as its denial is self-contradictory,
it shows that there is no room for any doubt about *it* for God to
remove. It also shows that any doubt about intuitions *in general*

---

[33] I believe that the opacity between a proposition with regard to its type
only (doubting 'in general') and with regard to it as a particular instance (doubting 'in particular') is equivalent for Descartes to the opacity between two
different general descriptions of the same proposition. This follows from the
fact that particular propositions which are clearly and distinctly perceived are
also seen to be instances of the general type which I cannot doubt.

will be removed by something that they all share *qua* intuitions (viz., that their opposites are contradictions and therefore cannot be doubted), instead of being removed by something peculiar to one intuition (viz., that God is non-deceptive). Thus, the *cogito* is the vindicating intuition in a somewhat accidental way, i.e., it happened to be the first available intuition. The *cogito* also has a logical primacy amongst intuitions since any other intuition can be prefaced by 'I think. . . .'

C. *The metaphysical doubt is an odd sort of doubt.* But whether or not one agrees with my thesis about the doubt is removable independently of any appeal to God's existence, the doubt itself needs some discussion. This need arises when one wonders what the doubt amounts to. If we suppose that Descartes has not yet removed the doubt, what does he lack? He does not lack certainty about the truth of any intuition he considers while considering it, so he must lack such certainty while *not* considering it. This means that the metaphysical doubt is a *doubt by inattention*.

This way of describing it sheds some light on his explicit intention to doubt only conclusions whose premises have been forgotten. Both the doubt of intuitions in general and the doubt of conclusions (without premises) are doubts by inattention; they only differ in what *is* attended to. In the former, one attends to the rule only and in the latter, one attends to a particular conclusion only.

But what can happen to an intuition (or a premise) when one is not attending to it? Whether anything happens to an intuition or not, Descartes may just be worried that something might happen. As Kenny was quoted earlier as saying, 'To engage in metaphysical doubt is . . . to betray the weakness of the human intellect that is incapable of holding intuitions steady.' If the doubt is a purely human weakness like a neurotic anxiety, then the removal of the doubt by God is akin to therapy by a trustworthy friend in that nothing changes except our attitude towards intuitions while not attending to them. But if it is not neurotic, but well-founded, then it must be based on something about intuitions themselves and not merely our attitude toward them. The only possibility is that all we know for certain is that they are true while under consideration. We do not know that the truth-values of intuitions do not change while we are not presently attending to them. This presents the metaphysical doubt as a sort of 'problem of induction', an uncertainty about whether perceived truths remain true even while no longer being perceived.

Either we try to show that the doubt is empty because intuitions are necessary truths and leave no room for a change of truth-values, or we appeal to God's free but good will to 'hold them steady'. Unfortunately, the latter appeal begs the issue, since the intuition of God may (for all we know) change while we are not attending to it and turn up false the next time we consider it.

Finally, then, what can we conclude about the criterion, the doubt, and the circle? I believe I have shown that the criterion of truth is not clarity and distinctness *simpliciter*, but the clarity and distinctness of necessary truth. If this is true, then there need be no circle of any kind involving the metaphysical doubt and the intuition of God's existence as a non-deceptive creator, since the rule needs no justification when applied to propositions in particular nor in general (R3").

If we discount this analysis of the rule, there is still no circle about individual intuitions while attending to them, since they are indubitable and need no justification at all (R3'). Whether or not the metaphysical 'doubt by inattention' yields a circle will depend on how one understands the doubt. If it is only a neurotic fear, then there is no circle, since Gods' function is therapeutic, not justificatory. If it is more than this, and implies that God's role is justificatory, then there is indeed a genuine Cartesian Circle. But since I do not have a clear and distinct perception of any truth about the nature of the metaphysical doubt, I cannot conclude for certain that there is a circle nor that there is none, only that there need not be one.

VII

THE RELIABILITY OF REASON

STANLEY TWEYMAN

In the first meditation Descartes seeks to show that two different hypotheses—that of a deceiving deity and that of a malignant demon—stand as obstacles to gaining knowledge. Accordingly, each must be dealt with, for until this is done the reliability of reason remains suspect; that is, only in this manner can Descartes show that reason is able to set up canons for its own trustworthiness. The concern of this paper will be to determine just how Descartes carries out this programme.

Several commentators have held that the indubitability of the *Cogito* destroys the hypothesis of the evil genius since the demon was imagined to possess full powers of deception.[1] As everyone knows, the *Cogito* is uncovered in the second meditation when Descartes begins his quest for at least one thing which can withstand his hyperbolic doubt; for no matter how much he doubts his former beliefs, he cannot at the same time doubt his existence. Now, since Descartes' own existence was not called into question in the first meditation, the extent of the deceptive powers there attributed to the evil genius are in no way affected by the *Cogito*, and consequently, the recognition of the *Cogito* does not, by itself, disprove this hypothesis.[2] Besides, Descartes' usual mode of speaking about the evil genius does not support the view being examined: he usually speaks of the evil genius as employing his

[1] For example Beck writes: 'The force of the hypothesis of the Malignant Spirit breaks on the rock of the *Cogito*. The recognition of one truth as indubitably true, and self-evidently so, gives a rational conviction which is sufficient to destroy the hypothesis once for all. The *Cogito* destroys the very basis of the postulate of an all-powerful deceiving being' (L. J. Beck, *The Metaphysics of Descartes* (Oxford, 1965), p. 143). Similarly Versfeld states: 'His [i.e. the evil genius's] essence was to possess full powers of deception. Without that he is nothing. The evil genius, then, disappears with the affirmation of the *Cogito*'. (M. Versfeld, *An Essay on the Metaphysics of Descartes* (London, 1940), p. 49).

[2] It is also abundantly clear that in the first meditation Descartes already possessed the knowledge of one truth, namely, that by suspending his judgment he cannot be imposed upon by the evil genius. Therefore, if any truth indubitably known were sufficient to shatter the evil genius hypothesis, then Descartes already possessed a knowledge of it before he came to the *Cogito*.

whole energies in deceiving him,[3] and not as necessarily possessing full powers of deception. As such, it is a non sequitur to conclude that the recognition of the *Cogito* disproves the hypothesis, for the evil genius may not be able to deceive him in regard to this matter, and yet be able to do so in others. The recognition of the *Cogito* shows a limit to the evil genius's power, but it does not disprove his existence. Putting the matter generally, we can say that what Descartes wants to know is not only whether the evil genius possesses full powers of deception, but also whether he possesses any at all, and it simply will not do to try to answer this latter question with a reply to the former. Therefore, to disprove this hypothesis more is needed than the indubitability of the *Cogito*.

Two passages in the text support this interpretation:

> But there is some deceiver or other, very powerful and very cunning who employs his ingenuity in deceiving me. Then without doubt I exist also if he deceives me, and *let him deceive me as much as he will*, he can never cause me to be nothing so long as I think I am something.[4]
> But what am I, now that I suppose that there is a certain genius which is extremely powerful, and, if I may say so, malicious, who employs all his powers in deceiving me.[5]

The italicized portion of the first passage is significant because, being spoken at the point at which Descartes first recognizes the indubitability of the *Cogito*, it confirms the continued viability of the evil genius hypothesis. The second passage is important inasmuch as it appears after the recognition of the *Cogito* when Descartes is concerned with making the self an object of thought in order to determine what he is now that he knows that he is. Yet even here he is still entertaining the possibility of being deceived by the evil genius.

The view of the evil genius discussed above can be called the postulational view; that is, Descartes has postulated the evil genius as existing independently of himself. The text, however, can also support an alternative interpretation. If the synopsis of the first meditation[6] is read in conjunction with the concluding paragraphs

[3] See, e.g., HR I, 148.
[4] HR I, 150 (my italics).
[5] HR I, 151.
[6] HR I, 140.

of the first meditation it becomes clear that the evil genius embodies those very functions which Descartes attributes to hyperbolic doubt, namely, the ability to unprejudice the mind, and to set the mind on the path of acquiring knowledge. Accordingly, the evil genius can also be regarded as merely personifying his hyperbolic doubt—a device just as effective as that of postulating the existence of a malignant being in that both help to emphasize the present uncertainty in his opinions. Since the hypothesis is susceptible to these two interpretations it is important to see how Descartes deals with each. At this stage of the argument, however, the indubitability of the *Cogito* is no more able to destroy the personification view than it is able to destroy the postulation view. The personification view will be destroyed when the continued viability of hyperbolic doubt is removed, and this requires more than the *Cogito* as it is apprehended in the second meditation.

That more than the *Cogito* is required to treat satisfactorily of the evil genius hypothesis[7] should occasion no surprise, for the Cartesian enterprise as presented in the first two meditations is a systematic attempt through the use of this hypothesis to search for but one thing which is indubitable, or to convince himself that such a thing cannot be found.[8] Hence, there is no need at this stage to try to disprove the evil genius hypothesis if—as he found to be the case—the hypothesis itself is instrumental in uncovering this one certain thing. Descartes' success with the *Cogito* impelled him in the third meditation to examine this first instant of knowing with a view to acquiring even more knowledge. We shall see that it is this enlarged enterprise which forces Descartes to consider a final solution to the problem of the evil genius.

By reflecting on the *Cogito* Descartes sought to determine what it was that convinced him of its truth. His considered view was that

in this first knowledge there is nothing that assures me of its truth, excepting the clear and distinct perception of that which I state, which would not indeed suffice to assure me that what I say is true, if it could even happen that a thing which I conceived so clearly and distinctly could be false; and accordingly it seems to me that I can establish as a general rule that all things which I perceive very clearly and very distinctly are true.[9]

---

[7] From this point on, I will refer to the hypothesis of the evil genius to cover both interpretations discussed when it is not necessary to make a distinction between them.

[8] HR I, 149.   [9] HR I, 158.

It should be noticed that Descartes is not questioning whether the *Cogito* is perceived clearly and distinctly, nor whether the *Cogito* is true. Beyond this, however, Descartes' meaning is far from clear.

The passage above can be taken to mean that Descartes is not yet convinced that whatever is perceived clearly and distinctly is true simply because the truth of the *Cogito* was apprehended through the fact that it it was perceived clearly and distinctly. Accordingly, to show that whatever is perceived clearly and distinctly is true it must be shown that nothing which is perceived clearly and distinctly can be false. The reason for doubting the truth of the principle concerning clarity and distinctness is said to be the possibility of a deceiving deity who could 'cause me to err, even in matters in which I believe myself to have the best evidence.'[10] That is, so long as I am attending to something which is very clearly and very distinctly perceived, I am entirely persuaded of its truth.[11] However, after I cease attending to it, I can, through the employment of hyperbolic doubt, consider that even in this persuasion I was deceived since I can entertain the possibility of a deity who deceives me into believing that what I am perceiving clearly and distinctly is true, whereas in actual fact it is false. The *Cogito* has withstood the doubts caused by these reflections, but yet if he is ever to be certain of any other truth he must go on to prove that there is a deity who is not a deceiver. If he succeeds in this then the *Cogito* is shown to be the unconditional paradigm of knowledge, and the reliability of reason is established.

It is this interpretation of the matter at which Arnauld and others arrived in an effort to understand the role of the divine guarantee. Such an attempt, however, was held to be circular for the very criterion employed in proving God's existence was to be guaranteed by the proof itself:

The only remaining scruple I have is an uncertainty as to how a circular reasoning is to be avoided in saying: the only secure reason we have for believing that what we clearly and distinctly

---

[10] Ibid.

[11] 'And even although I had not demonstrated this (viz. all that I clearly know is true) the nature of my mind is such that I could not prevent myself from holding them to be true so long as I conceive them clearly'. (HR I, 180) '. . . it is only those things we conceive clearly and distinctly that have the power of persuading me entirely.' (HR I, 183). See also Principle XLIII.

perceive is true, is the fact that God exists. But we can be sure that God exists only because we clearly and evidently perceive that; therefore prior to being certain that God exists, we should be certain that whatever we clearly and evidently perceive is true.[12]

In response to Arnauld's charge, Descartes says that 'we are sure that God exists because we have attended to the proofs that established this fact, but afterwards it is enough for us to remember that we have perceived something clearly in order to be sure that it is true, but this would not suffice, unless we knew that God existed and that he did not deceive us.'[13] Further clarification of his position is offered in the replies to the second set of objections[14] wherein Descartes maintains that the persuasion attending matters seen very clearly and very distinctly is tantamount to perfect certitude. As a result, the truth of such matters cannot be doubted. There are other matters, however, which are perceived very clearly and very distinctly so long as we attend to the reasons leading us to them, 'but since we can forget those reasons and yet remember the conclusions deduced from them, the question is raised whether we can entertain the same firm and immutable certainty as to these conclusions, during the time that we recollect that they have been deduced from first principles that are evident; for this remembrance must be assumed in order that they may be called conclusions.'[15] In other words, the divine guarantee concerns the reliability of memory in the case of valid demonstrations as opposed to the truth of what is now being perceived clearly and distinctly.

As so interpreted, Arnauld's change is out of place, since the scope of hyperbolic doubt extends only to the memory of valid demonstrations.[16] However, unless Descartes can show that there is no employment of memory in proving God's existence, the charge of circular reasoning will again be applicable. There are at least two passages in the *Meditations* which indicate that the employment of memory is not required in proving God's existence.

[12] HR II, 92.
[13] HR II, 115.
[14] See especially HR II, 38, 41–3.
[15] HR II, 42–3.
[16] The points to be made in the remainder of the article will not require a review of the proofs for the existence of God in the third meditation. I am assuming that the reader has some familiarity with them.

The first occurs in the third meditation immediately after the first line of argument for God's existence has been presented. He says that 'to speak the truth, I see nothing in all that I have just said which by the light of nature is not manifest to anyone who desires to think attentively on the subject, but when I slightly relax my attention . . . I do not easily recollect the reason why the idea I possess of a being more perfect than I, must necessarily have been placed in me by a being which is really more perfect.'[17] Similarly, in the fifth meditation he says that 'for a firm grasp of this truth [viz. that God exists] I have need of a strenuous application of mind.'[18] Therefore, so long as one attends to the proof memory need not be employed, and there is no possibility of circular reasoning.

Even so, a further difficulty presents itself, because although Descartes can be assured of the existence of God while attending to the proof, he must, if the charge of circular reasoning is to be avoided again, show that even when he is not attending to the proof, the knowledge of God's existence is in no way dependent on memory; for if it is, then it cannot be employed to dispel his doubts about the reliability of memory. Thus far the *Cogito* alone has been able to withstand hyperbolic doubt. Certain passages following the proofs for God's existence in the third meditation, however, indicate that Descartes holds that the idea of God is contained in the intuition of the self.

> . . . when I reflect on myself I not only know that I am something incomplete and dependent on another, which incessantly aspires after something which is better and greater than myself, but I also know that he on whom I depend possesses in himself all the great things towards which I aspire, and that not indefinitely or potentially alone, but really, actually and infinitely; and that thus he is God.[19]
> And when I consider that I doubt, that is to say, that I am an incomplete and dependent being, the idea of a being that is complete and independent, that is of God, presents itself to my mind, with so much distinctness and clearness—that I do not think that the human mind is capable of knowing anything with more evidence and certitude.[20]

[17] HR I, 167.　　　　　　　　[18] HR I, 183.
[19] HR I, 170.　　　　　　　　[20] HR I, 171–2.

Once one attends to the proofs for the existence of God the mind is led to see the incomplete nature of the intuition of the self as it was previously apprehended, for it is now clear that this intuition is also capable of revealing the true God upon which he and whatever else which exists depends. The proofs for the existence of God, therefore, only serve as a didactic device to unprejudice the mind so far as the existence of God is concerned, and to lead the mind to a fuller appreciation of the original intuition. Consequently, there is no circle here either, for ultimately knowledge of God is obtained through the *Cogito*, and the latter as we have seen escapes all hyperbolic doubt.

From the fact that the existence of a veracious God has been established, it does not follow that there is no possibility of deception with regard to any other matter. Descartes himself realized this early in the fourth Meditation:

> And no doubt respecting this matter would remain, if it were not that the consequences would seem to follow that I can thus never be deceived; for if I hold all that I possess from God, and if He has not placed in me the capacity for error, it seems as though I could never fall into error—[but] experience shows me that I am nevertheless subject to an infinitude of errors—[21]

Accordingly, it is at this point that Descartes will deal with the evil genius hypothesis—the second hypothesis charged with being an obstacle to knowing, and in fact that hypothesis which has sustained his suspense of judgment—and do so in such a way that this hypothesis will never again threaten his knowing anything. Since the fourth meditation is largely concerned with discovering the nature and source of error, it is through an examination of this topic that Descartes' treatment of the evil genius is revealed. On the nature of deception and error he writes:

> Whence then come my errors? They come from the sole fact that since the will is much wider in its range and compass than the understanding, I do not restrain it within the same bounds, but extend it also to things which I do not understand: and as the will is of itself indifferent to these, it easily falls into error and sin, and chooses the evil for the good, or the false for the true.[22]

[21] HR I, 172.
[22] HR I, 175–6.

Concerning the source of error he asserts:

> But if I abstain from giving my judgment on any thing when I
> do not perceive it with sufficient clearness and distinctness, it
> is plain that I act rightly and am not deceived. But if I determine
> to deny or affirm, I no longer make use as I should of my free
> will, and if I affirm what is not true, it is evident that I deceive
> myself—[23]

In addition, this knowledge of the source of error can be immunized
from hyperbolic doubt:

> He [i.e. God] has at least left [it] within my power—to adhere
> to the resolution never to give judgment on matters whose
> truth is not clearly known to me; for although I notice a certain
> weakness in my nature in that I cannot continually concentrate
> my mind on one single thought, I can yet, by attentive and
> frequently repeated meditation, impress it so forcibly on my
> memory that I shall never fail to recollect it whenever I have
> need of it, and thus acquire the habit of never going astray.[24]

If Descartes intended to postulate a being existing independently
of himself when he introduced the evil genius, then in dealing
with such a being he has but two alternatives: he must show either
that such a being cannot exist, or if he cannot do this he must
establish that even if such a being does exist, he is rendered
irrelevant to Descartes' argument. Now the most that has been
accomplished through gaining knowledge of the source of error is
to find a way of immunizing himself from the evil genius, if such
a being exists. For he now knows that so long as he does not extend
his will beyond his understanding, he cannot be imposed upon by
such a being. Nowhere in the *Meditations*, however, does Descartes show that if God exists the evil genius cannot exist; in
other words, Descartes has not established that the universe
cannot be dualistic, which is what is required if the non-existence
of the evil genius is to be shown.

If, on the other hand, the evil genius is employed as the
personification of hyperbolic doubt, this hypothesis will be
destroyed if and only if the purpose for the doubt itself is removed.
Hyperbolic doubt was introduced in the first meditation to
prevent Descartes from assenting to what is false while he was

[23] HR I, 176.   [24] HR I, 178.

ignorant of how to distinguish the true from the false. Since knowledge of how to make this distinction is obtained in the fourth meditation, hyperbolic doubt need no longer be employed. Thus at the beginning of the fifth meditation he writes:

> Now (after first noting what must be done or avoided, in order to arrive at a knowledge of the truth) my principal task is to endeavour to emerge from the state of doubt into which I have these last days fallen—[25]

Having now shown that God exists and cannot be a deceiver, and having also shown that the evil genius hypothesis will never again be troublesome, the reliability of reason has been established for he can now accept the general rule that whatever is perceived very clearly and very distinctly is true:

> In the fourth *Meditation* it is shown that all these things which we very clearly and distinctly perceive are true—[26]

Thus when he asserts in the third meditation that his acceptance of this rule depends only on proving that God is not a deceiver, this must be considered a stage in his argument and not his final pronouncement on the subject.

Having now discussed how Descartes establishes the reliability of reason when hyperbolic doubt extends to the memory of valid demonstrations, I now proceed to examine how the reliability of reason can be established if hyperbolic doubt is regarded as covering what is clearly and distinctly perceived. To this end I shall examine again the charge of circular reasoning in proving God's existence, and I shall also consider the possibility in the fourth meditation of circular reasoning in establishing the principle that whatever is perceived very clearly and very distinctly is true.

Since hyperbolic doubt now extends to principles which are perceived clearly and distinctly, it appears that Arnauld's charge of circular reasoning is well founded. However, Descartes had a way of avoiding this difficulty. What throws doubt on the demonstration of God's existence is that the demonstration may entirely persuade us in so far as each step is seen clearly and distinctly and yet it may lead to a false conclusion. The truth of the conclusion could be established, however, if there were

[25] HR I, 179.
[26] HR I, 142; see also HR I, 140.

K

an additional factor which was not only known to be true, but also showed conclusively that the demonstration itself is altogether trustworthy. Since the *Cogito* is the only truth which has managed to escape hyperbolic doubt, it is to it that we must look as the guarantor of the soundness of this demonstration.

We have already examined two passages in which Descartes holds that once one attends to the proof of God's existence it becomes manifest that the idea of God is contained in the original intuition of the self, and consequently by attending to this intuition one is assured of God's existence as well as the existence of the self. Accordingly, the truth of the conclusion is established by the fact that the conclusion is contained in the original intuition of the self—an intuition already accepted as true. In addition, since it is not solely because each premise was seen clearly and distinctly that the conclusion is accepted, there can be no circle here. Only if the original intuition contained no more than an apprehension of the self would the proofs for God's existence in the third meditation be circular and valueless.

It cannot be emphasized too strongly that it is in the fourth meditation and not in the third that Descartes claims to have established the principle that whatever is perceived clearly and distinctly is true. The synopsis to the fourth meditation also indicates that Descartes holds that the truth of this principle has been established 'at the same time—[as]—it is explained in what the nature of error or falsity consists'.[27] We saw that error arises through allowing the will to extend beyond the understanding, i.e. from assenting to matters which the understanding does not perceive clearly and distinctly. However, if this explanation is based solely on the fact that its truth is seen clearly and distinctly then Descartes' attempt to establish the principle that whatever is perceived clearly and distinctly is true is circular. Therefore, if this principle is to survive it must be based on something other than merely perceiving it clearly and distinctly.

One passage indicates that Descartes intends to found his knowledge of the source of error on the fact that it is seen clearly and distinctly:

—the light of nature teaches us that the knowledge of the understanding should always precede the determination of the will.[28]

[27] HR I, 142.   [28] HR I, 176.

In other places he claims that the principle in question has actually been demonstrated.[29] Guidance in locating his demonstration is provided by a passage in the fifth meditation:

> But after I have recognized that there is a God—because at the same time I have also recognized that all things depend upon Him, and that he is not a deceiver, and from that have inferred what I perceive clearly and distinctly cannot fail to be true—[30]

According to this passage establishing the principle in question requires showing first that there is a veracious God upon whom all things depend and then that there is an inference from this knowledge to the truth of the principle concerning clarity and distinctness.

As this argument stands it is an enthymeme, and the premise required to validate it is found in the fourth meditation. In the last paragraph he explains that

> every clear and distinct conception is without doubt something, and hence cannot derive its origin from what is nought but must of necessity have God as its author.[31]

Therefore Descartes' full argument for the truth of the principle that whatever is perceived clearly and distinctly is true is:

I   There exists a non-deceiving God upon whom all things depend.

II   Every clear and distinct perception is something.

∴III   Every clear and distinct perception must have God as its author.

∴ IV   There can be no deception concerning any clear and distinct idea.

∴ V   What I perceive clearly and distinctly cannot fail to be true.

It is this argument which dispels the fear expressed early in the third meditation that a clear and distinct idea might be false. There is, as it were, an alliance established between God and the self so that the problem of the evil genius and that of error need

---

[29] '. . . I have already fully demonstrated that all that I know clearly is true.' (HR I, 180) See also HR I, 140.
[30] HR I, 184.
[31] For further comment on this passage see HR I, 105.

never arise again. What is equally important is that the principle concerning the truth of clear and distinct ideas has been established without circularity since it is not accepted merely because it is apprehended with clarity and distinctness.[32]

Even though the arguments in the first meditation threatened the reliability of reason, by the end of the fourth meditation Descartes claims to have established that reason can prove its own reliability through its ability to establish the existence of a veracious God. In response to this attempt to establish the reliability of reason Frankfurt writes:[33]

> But Descartes' reasoning may well be defective and it may even be circular. Indeed, the following serious question must be raised about it. Given that reason leads to the conclusion that reason is reliable because a veracious God exists, may it not also lead to the conclusion that there is an omnipotent demon whose existence renders reason unreliable? Of course, these conclusions are incompatible, and if the proper use of reason established both of them it would mean that reason is unreliable. But surely Descartes cannot take for granted that this is not the case. His procedure does, therefore, seem to beg the question, though in a rather different way than has generally been thought.[34]

Let 'P' stand for 'reason concludes that a varacious God exists', 'R' stand for 'reason concludes that an omnipotent demon exists'[35] and 'Q' stand for 'reason is reliable'. We can then symbolize Frankfurt's claim concerning what Descartes has established as follows:

[32] In the *Reply to Objections II* Descartes offers another proof for the truth of this principle based on the fact that God is not a deceiver and that all things stem from God. He argues there that since we can imagine no other correct use of our faculty for distinguishing truth from falsehood than to assent only to clear and distinct perceptions, and since this faculty has been given to us by God, what is clearly and distinctly perceived must be true, or God can be charged with being a deceiver (HR II, 42). This proof also escapes all charges of circularity.

[33] H. G. Frankfurt, 'Descartes' Validation of Reason', *The American Philosophical Quarterly*, II (1965), pp. 148–156.

[34] Ibid., footnote 22.

[35] Since my paper has shown that Descartes has not necessarily established that non-existence of the evil genius although he has established the way of immunizing himself from all error, in the context of my paper 'R' must be understood to represent 'the reliability of reason is threatened by the possibility of the evil genius'.

$(P \supset Q). (R \supset \sim Q)$
P
_____

Therefore Q

However, in order to establish conclusively the reliability of reason Descartes had to establish a second premise containing not only 'P' but the conjunction of 'P' with '$\sim R$,' for only in this way can it be shown that reason will not lead to 'Q and $\sim Q$'. That is, according to Frankfurt Descartes had to show that

$(P \supset Q). (R \supset \sim Q)$
P. $\sim R$
_____

Therefore Q

Otherwise, Descartes merely supposes but never establishes that reason will not lead to

$(P \supset Q). (R \supset \sim Q)$
P. R
_____

Therefore Q. $\sim Q$

Accordingly, in proving that reason is reliable Descartes is assuming that reason is consistent; but since part of establishing the reliability of reason rests on proving reason consistent, it appears that Descartes is begging the question he is attempting to answer.

The *Meditations*, however, does not contain the *petitio principii* for which Frankfurt argues. Descartes holds that reason is reliable if it can be established that whatever is perceived clearly and distinctly is true, and the truth of this principle is established by proving that a veracious God exists. That Descartes has actually established the consistency of reason is clear from the fact that the *Cogito* is consistent.

> Let who will deceive me, He can never cause me to be nothing while I think that I am, or some day cause—any such thing to be true in which I see a manifest contradiction.[36]

[36] HR I, 158–9. Similarly in *Principle* VII he writes: 'We cannot in the same way conceive that we who doubt these things are not; for there is a contradiction in conceiving that what thinks does not at the same time as it thinks, exist. And hence this conclusion *I think, therefore I am*, is the first and most certain of all that occurs to one who philosophizes in an orderly way.' (HR I, 221)

Since knowledge of God's existence ultimately depends not on argument but on grasping the fullness of the *Cogito*, and since there is no contradiction in the *Cogito*, it follows that if the *Cogito*, supports a belief in the existence of a veracious God, which in turn establishes the reliability of reason, it is logically impossible for the *Cogito* to support any conclusion which would render the reliability of reason suspect. Therefore, once Descartes showed that the *Cogito* leads to the conclusion that a veracious God exists he believed himself to have established the reliability of reason. We can say that it was the *Cogito* which assured him that by establishing 'P' he had also established ' ∼ R'.

VIII

ON THE NON-EXISTENCE OF CARTESIAN LINGUISTICS

W. Keith Percival

In a number of recent monographs Chomsky has attempted to demonstrate the existence of an intellectual movement for which he has suggested the name 'Cartesian Linguistics'.[1] According to Chomsky this movement is responsible for the universal grammars which appeared in France beginning with the famous Port Royal Grammar of 1660 and culminating in the work of du Marsais in the eighteenth century. It is also responsible for many of the linguistic notions basic to the writings of Herder, Wilhelm von Humboldt, and August Wilhelm von Schlegel. Chomsky locates the major stimulus setting this movement going in certain remarks made by Descartes in the *Discourse on Method* and feels justified, therefore, in applying the epithet 'Cartesian' to the movement. However, in proposing this term Chomsky is careful to point out that he does not claim that all the representatives of the movement, from the Gentlemen of Port Royal to the German Romantics, felt themselves to be followers of Descartes in the philosophical sense.[2] With this reservation, then, Chomsky regards the term 'Cartesian Linguistics' as appropriate.

I shall not argue here that the term is inappropriate, but rather that Chomsky has not demonstrated that an intellectual movement such as he has in mind really ever existed, call it whatever you will. For a number of crucial historical assumptions are involved here which can be seen to be highly questionable once they are brought out into the open. The first of these historical assumptions is that Descartes' statements about language represent a novel departure from the traditional position. The second is that Descartes' ideas about language influenced the writers of universal grammars in fundamental respects. The

---

[1] See in particular *Cartesian Linguistics* (New York, 1966) and *Language and Mind* (New York, 1968).
[2] *Cartesian Linguistics*, pp. 75ff.

138   W. KEITH PERCIVAL

third assumption, and one which I shall not have time to go into
in this paper, is that the whole movement which Chomsky
designates by the term 'Cartesian Linguistics' forms a reasonably
homogeneous whole.

The important facts to establish then are the following:

1. Was what Descartes said about language in some interesting
sense different from, and let us say, more insightful than anything
that had been said before?

2. Were the universal grammarians crucially influenced by
Descartes?

Let us start with the first of these two questions and review
what beliefs Chomsky ascribes to Descartes with respect to
language. According to Chomsky, Descartes was the first to
champion 'the creative aspect of language use'. By the expression
'the created aspect of language use' Chomsky means the following
three things. First, that the normal use of language is innovative.
Second, that speech is free from the control of detectable stimuli,
either external or internal. And third, that utterances are appropriate to the situations in which they are uttered.[3]

Let us now examine Descartes' own statements to discover
whether he can be said to have believed in the creative aspect of
language use in the sense that Chomsky has in mind. How did
Descartes characterize human language, and what place did it
occupy in his general scheme of things? Let me recall a few
basic facts about Descartes' general philosophical position. He
considered, first of all, that there are two and only two kinds of
creative substance, namely, spiritual and corporeal. Living
bodies, he reasoned, are obviously not in the class of spiritual
substances. On the other hand, the human soul is something
which can hardly be ascribed to the class of corporeal substances.
Human beings, then, are creatures which are in some sense both
corporeal and spiritual, while inanimate nature is squarely in the
corporeal sphere. But what of animate nature other than the
human species? Here the decisive point is provided by Descartes'
conception of the soul as a substance whose principal attribute is
thinking, the capacity for thought. Human beings are the only
living creatures capable of thought; hence they are the only

[3] The clearest exposition of what Chomsky means by 'the creative aspect of
language use' is to be found in *Language and Mind*, pp. 10ff. See also *Cartesian
Linguistics*, pp. 3ff.

creatures which have immortal souls. Descartes' conclusion therefore is that the whole realm of animate nature apart from the human species must be relegated to the sphere of corporeal substance. Animals then are in essence no different from machines.

So, on the psychological level the crucial difference between man and the rest of animate nature is that man is capable of thought and animals are not. But thought, the activity of the soul, is unobservable, as indeed is spiritual substance itself. Hence the absence of such an activity cannot be ascertained by the senses. But thought is expressed and conveyed from one human being to another by means of language. Where linguistic behavior takes place, therefore, the creatures exhibiting this kind of behavior betray themselves as endowed with immortal souls. That animals are not so endowed is clearly shown by the fact that they do not indulge in linguistic behavior.

Obviously, however, animals are not completely devoid of communicative skills, and some of them can even be trained to produce reasonable imitations of human speech. Hence in order to show convincingly that animals do not think, and are not endowed with immortal souls, it is necessary for Descartes to distinguish between animal communication and human language, or at least to define what he means by 'true discourse' (*vera loquela*), to use Descartes' own term. In a letter to the English Platonist, Henry More, dated February 5, 1649, Descartes faced the problem in the following way: 'No animal', he says, 'has attained a degree of perfection such that it can use true discourse (*vera loquela*), that is to say, indicate something either by using its voice or by nodding, which could be ascribed to thought alone rather than to natural impulse.'[4] True discourse, in other words, occurs when a communicative act takes place which must be ascribed to thought and nothing else.

Note the curious circularity of the argument. A creature has a soul only if it is capable of using true discourse; discourse is of the genuine variety only if it can be ascribed to thought alone, thought being an activity which can be carried out only by a creature with a soul! Clearly if this latter were the only characteristic of true discourse, Descartes' discussion would be completely uninformative. However, he does present a somewhat fuller picture

---

[4]AT V, 278. Note that Chomsky cites this same passage from Descartes' letter to Henry More in *Cartesian Linguistics*, p. 6.

of human language in the Fifth Part of the *Discourse on Method*.⁵
The following characteristics of speech are mentioned in that
work:

1. Words reveal thoughts.⁶

2. True speech differs completely from natural cries in that it
does not indicate corporeal impulses.⁷

3. Words used in true discourse are not merely sounds
repeated by rote, but are directly expressive of thoughts.⁸

Let me pause here to point out that all the characteristics so
far enumerated reduce to the proposition that words reveal
thoughts *and nothing more*, as Descartes expressed it in his letter
to More many years later. But let me add one final characteristic
of human language mentioned by Descartes in the *Discourse on
Method*:

4. In genuine human discourse, what a person says is appropriate to 'whatever is said in his presence', or is 'relevant to the
subjects at hand'.⁹

Note in this connection that we are not told anything about
the range of possible 'subjects at hand', nor do we know in what
the relevance of utterances to subjects at hand consists. Let me
pursue this point a little further since this fourth characteristic
is the only one which removes Descartes' theory of language from
the level of vicious circularity. It is tempting to speculate that
what Descartes meant by 'relevance to subjects at hand' was
'logical connection'. Hence Descartes may be thought to be

---

⁵ See AT VI, 55–9, 571–3. For an English translation of this passage see
HR I, 116–7.

⁶ Descartes uses the expression *déclarer nos pensées* (*cogitationes nostras
aperire* in the Latin version of the *Discourse on Method* which he himself
authorized), AT VI, 56, line 22, and AT VI, 571.

⁷ AT VI, 58, line 16, and AT VI, 572. The Latin version is especially clear
on this point: 'Notandumque est loquelam, signaque omnia quae ex hominum
instituto cogitationes significant, plurimum differre a vocibus et signis naturali-
bus quibus corporei affectus indicantur' AT VI, 572.

⁸ AT VI, 57, line 25, and AT VI, 572. Here Descartes points out that
although Magpies and parrots are capable of uttering the same words as we do,
they are nevertheless unable to speak like us, that is to say, in such a way as to
show that they understand what they are saying: ". . . videmus enim picas et
psittacos easdem quas nos voces proferre, nec tamen sicut nos loqui posse, hoc
est, ita ut ostendant se intelligere quid dicant."

⁹ AT VI, 56, line 30, and AT VI, 572. In this passage Descartes imagines
a machine built to resemble a human being outwardly and so designed internally
that it is able to produce a different utterance depending on how its various parts
are manipulated from outside. Such a machine, Descartes believes, would still
be distinguishable from a real human being in that it would be unable to put
words together in response to whatever might be said in its presence.

claiming that what a person says is logically connected to the subject at hand.

This is quite a plausible interpretation in the light of some other remarks he makes in the same passage of the *Discourse on Method*. Here he contrasts human reason on the one hand, and the faculties animals are endowed with on the other, pointing out that, unlike animal capacities, reason is a 'universal instrument which can function in all kinds of situations'. However, he goes on to point out the fact that even the most stupid human being is fully capable of using genuine language, and that even the most gifted animal is incapable of the same, and infers from this that very little reason is required to be able to speak, and that animals have no reason whatever.

A similar argument is developed in a letter Descartes wrote to the Marquis of Newcastle, dated November 23, 1646. In this letter he asserts that none of our external actions offers more convincing evidence that 'there is a soul in us which has thoughts' than the fact that we use words appropriately to the matter at issue. He then goes on to say that he emphasizes the notion of appropriateness in order to make it clear that parrots are incapable of true speech, but that madmen are, since although what a madman says is devoid of reason it is nevertheless relevant to the subject at hand.[10] Clearly then Descartes' notion of the appropriateness of utterances means no more than that what we say is always related to a subject matter which includes more than the meaning of the particular sentence being uttered.

At this point let us glance back at Chomsky's three defining attributes of the creative aspect of language use, namely (1) innovativeness, (2) freedom from the control of detectable stimuli, and (3) appropriateness to situations. Descartes obviously subscribed to the third of these notions. Concerning the second, 'freedom from the control of detectable stimuli', we must be careful not to confuse Descartes' and Chomsky's notions of the mind. Recall that Chomsky attacked behavioristic approaches to such problems as verbal behavior *on empirical grounds*.[11] Descartes,

---

[10] 'Je dis . . . que ces signes soient à propos, pour exclure le parler des perroquets, sans exclure celui des foux, qui ne laisse pas d'être à propos des sujets qui se présentent.' AT IV, 574.

[11] See Noam Chomsky, 'Review of B. F. Skinner, *Verbal Behavior*', *Language* 35 (1959), pp. 26–58, republished in J. A. Fodor and J. J. Katz (eds.), *The Structure of Language* (Englewood Cliffs, N. J., 1964), pp. 547–578.

on the other hand, had no behaviorists to contend with, and
refused to allow the soul to be subject to the laws of efficient
causation not merely for empirical reasons but, more importantly,
because of certain general philosophical positions he adopted,
notably the decision to dichotomize nature into corporeal and
spiritual substance. While the results of Descartes' and Chomsky's
trains of thought may seem superficially similar, the differences
between them are in reality profound.

Finally, the property of innovativeness which Chomsky
ascribes to the use of natural language is difficult to identify in
Descartes' explicit statements about human discourse. The
nearest thing to this notion is perhaps to be found in the implication of the universal quantifier in the phrase 'appropriate to
whatever is said in the speaker's presence' (from the *Discourse on
Method*).[12] It is just conceivable that Descartes realized that since
the number of possible questions is infinite, the number of
possible answers to them is also infinite. At all events, even if this
interpretation is forced on the text the notions of innovativeness
and potential unboundedness which are basic to Chomsky's
view of language play a negligible role in Descartes' discussion of
the subject.

As for the novelty of Descartes' positions, his critics concentrated
almost all their fire on his characterization of animals as machines,
rather than on his statements about the nature of language.[13]
After all, what Descartes said about language boils down to two
propositions: one, that language serves *no other function* than
to convey thoughts; and the other, that when a person says
something, there is some connection between what he says and
the general topic being discussed. The first of these is novel only
in the sense that at least some earlier theorists emphasized that
speech also has functions other than the obvious one of conveying
thought.[14] Descartes' theory, if it is to be considered novel at all,

[12]AT VI, 57, line 1 ('pour répondre au sens de *tout* ce qui se dira en sa
présence'). Emphasis mine.
    [13] See, for example, Henry More's letters to Descartes in the period 1648–49,
AT V, 244ff; 311.
    [14] See, for example, the discussion of Aquinas' views of language and its
various functions in Franz Manthey, *Die Sprachphilosophie des heiligen Thomas
von Aquin*, Paderborn, 1937, especially pp. 59–61. It may also be recalled that
Aristotle characterized speech as something which is accompanied by an act of
the imagination and is produced by a creature that has soul in it (*De anima* II,
8). Like Descartes he too insisted that speech does not exist merely to reveal
pleasure and pain (*Politics* I, 2).

represents rather a backward step from the teachings of previous centuries. The second of the two propositions, the one which concerns appropriateness, I have already pointed out, amounts to nothing more than a commonplace.

As regards the putative Cartesian origins of the Port Royal approach to universal grammar, a few brief critical remarks suggest themselves.

Chomsky claims, first of all, that in accordance with the Cartesian body-mind dichotomy the Port Royal grammarians assume that language has two aspects, sound and meaning.[15] Now it is true of course that Descartes himself would have dealt with the phonetic aspects of language in terms of corporeal substance, and the semantic aspects in terms of spiritual substance, if he had ever thought about the matter. The difficulty is, however, that all previous grammarians had treated language as having these aspects ever since language began to exercise the curiosity of man. To claim that Descartes is responsible for the Port Royal grammarians' distinguishing between sound and meaning, one would have to produce specific documentary evidence of Cartesian influence, which Chomsky has so far failed to do.

The second claim that Chomsky makes is that a distinction similar to that between deep and surface structure in his own grammatical theory was already drawn by the Port Royal grammarians, and attributes this again to their Cartesian approach. Whether in fact the Gentlemen of Port Royal can be said to have drawn such a distinction is a moot point which I cannot go into here,[16] but that such a notion could be the result of assimilating Descartes' ideas about language I find difficult to believe. Indeed, research by Gunvor Sahlin,[17] Robin Lakoff,[18] and Vivian Salmon[19]

[15] Chomsky, *Cartesian Linguistics*, p. 32.
[16] Briefly, Chomsky makes the mistake, in my view, of equating his notion of deep structure with the set of basic propositions, which, the Port Royal grammarians claimed, underlie complex sentences. I assume that for Chomsky a deep structure merely *determines* the semantic interpretation of a sentence. The Port Royal grammarians believed, on the other hand, that the set of underlying propositions was the same thing as the semantic interpretation of the sentence. For an interesting discussion of the difference between Chomsky's position and that of the Port Royal grammarians, see Karl E. Zimmer, "Review of *Cartesian Linguistics*", *International Journal of American Linguistics*, 34 (1968), pp. 290–303, especially 295ff.
[17] Gunvor Sahlin, *César Chesneau du Marsais et son rôle dans l'évolution de la Grammaire générale*, Paris, 1928.
[18] Robin Lakoff, 'Review of Herbert H. Brekle (ed.), *Grammaire Générale et Raisonnée*', *Language* 45 (1969), pp. 343–364. In this review Lakoff shows in what specific ways the writers of the Port Royal grammar were indebted to

has produced abundant evidence that the Port Royal theory of syntax rests on a tradition going back a good hundred years before the publication of the *Grammaire Générale*, namely the grammatical tradition represented by such works as the Elder Scaliger's *De Causis Linguae Latinae* of 1540 and Sanctius' *Minerva* of 1587. A component in this tradition which still awaits investigation is a type of pedagogically oriented universal grammar which began appearing in Germany about 1615, twenty years before Descartes published his first book.[20] That universal grammar began with Port Royal and had Cartesian origins is a hypothesis which sounds less and less plausible the more we learn about the development of linguistic theory since the Renaissance.

Finally, let me formulate my general conclusion in the following way: Chomsky has so far failed to show convincing proof that Descartes had any influence on the French universal grammarians of the late seventeenth century. Hence the term 'Cartesian Linguistics' would appear to be thoroughly misleading. It should be emphasized, however, that my arguments have not shown that Descartes had no impact whatever on grammatical theory. At present I lean toward the view that, unlike most of the other major philosophers of the seventeenth century, Descartes was relatively uninterested in language. It seems more likely therefore that the upsurge of interest in grammatical theory sprang from sources other than Descartes' philosophy. While I would be the last person to discourage attempts to demonstrate historical connections between philosophical and linguistic theorizing, the persistence of a long established grammatical tradition independent of the intellectual climate of each period has to be reckoned with. It goes without saying that this grammatical tradition itself has philosophical bases, though obviously of much greater antiquity than the ideas we have been concerned with in this paper.

Sanctius. Her analysis, however, suffers from the same historical naïveté as Chomsky betrays in *Cartesian Linguistics*. Like him she believes that current transformational linguistics has a historical origin separate from that of non-transformational linguistics. She differs from him in that she portrays Sanctius rather than Descartes or Lancelot as the founding father of transformational linguistics in the early modern period.

[19] See Vivian Salmon, 'Review of Noam Chomsky, *Cartesian Linguistics*', *Journal of Linguistics*, 5, No. 1, (1969), pp. 165–187.

[20] Max Jellinek provides some interesting information about these pedagogical general grammars in his monumental *Geschichte der neuhochdeutschen Grammatik*, (Heidelberg, 1913), vol. 1, pp. 88–94.

This conclusion should not, it seems to me, daunt the investigator, and it is greatly to Chomsky's credit that he has boldly advanced historical hypotheses which more pedestrian scholars would not have had the courage to publish. For in committing what might seem like an academic indiscretion, Chomsky has revealed the true extent of our present ignorance in this whole area.